The New York Times

PUBLIC PROFILES

Serial Killers

JACK THE RIPPER, SON OF SAM AND OTHERS

THE NEW YORK TIMES EDITORIAL STAFF

Published in 2019 by New York Times Educational Publishing
in association with The Rosen Publishing Group, Inc.
29 East 21st Street, New York, NY 10010

First Edition

The New York Times
Alex Ward: Editorial Director, Book Development
Phyllis Collazo: Photo Rights/Permissions Editor
Heidi Giovine: Administrative Manager

Rosen Publishing
Megan Kellerman: Managing Editor
Greg Tucker: Creative Director
Brian Garvey: Art Director

Cataloging-in-Publication Data
Names: New York Times Company.
Title: Serial killers: Jack the Ripper, Son of Sam and others /
edited by the New York Times editorial staff.
Description: New York : New York Times Educational Publishing,
2019. | Series: Public profiles | Includes glossary and index.
Identifiers: ISBN 9781642821789 (library bound) | ISBN
9781642821772 (pbk.) | ISBN 9781642821796 (ebook)
Subjects: LCSH: Serial murders—Juvenile literature. | Serial
murderers—Juvenile literature. | Serial murderers—Biography—
Juvenile literature. | Serial murders—Case studies—Juvenile
literature.
Classification: LCC HV6515.S47 2019 | DDC 364.152'32—dc23

Manufactured in the United States of America

On the cover: Mug shot of convicted New York City serial killer
David Berkowitz, known as Son of Sam; Hulton Archive/Stringer/
Archive Photos/Getty Images.

Contents

CHAPTER 3

Son of Sam: David Berkowitz

CHAPTER 4

John Wayne Gacy

CHAPTER 5

Jeffrey Dahmer

CHAPTER 6

B.T.K.: Dennis L. Rader

The Golden State Killer

Introduction

IT'S TRUE THAT some serial killers are exactly who people tend to think they are: white, dysfunctional, loner men motivated by sex who can't stop killing and who want to be caught. It's also true that some serial killers are black. Some are women. Some are motivated by greed, by anger or by the attention their acts receive in the media. Some serial killers are pillars of the community and others are pariahs. And some stop killing long before they are caught. But one thing all serial killers have in common is that they kill because they want to.

What causes someone to become a serial killer? It's hard to say for sure. But the common consensus among those who study serial killers — law enforcement officials, mental health professionals, academics and others — is that it's a combination of factors. In these uncommon individuals, biological, environmental, psychological and social dynamics develop in such a way that they have the desire to kill — and they decide to act on it.

Serial killers, although rare, have existed since ancient times. But public fascination with them began with a series of prostitute murders in the late 1880s in London's Whitechapel district. Committed by an unknown person who called himself "Jack the Ripper" in letters sent to the police, these grisly murders were reported in great detail, and news of them spread around the world. The killer was never caught, but the mythos of the serial killer was born.

The serial killers selected for this book, Jack the Ripper included, are among the most notorious. Their crimes were so unique or horrific that numerous articles were written about them. Each chapter profiles one killer — the murders, the hunt and in most cases, the capture, trial and sentencing — as told through articles published at the time of each event.

David Berkowitz, then the suspected "Son of Sam" killer, being taken into custody in Brooklyn in 1977.

Shortly after the excitement over Jack the Ripper's murders died down, stories of America's first serial killer, H. H. Holmes, began to circulate in the early 1890s. The police arrested Holmes for insurance fraud, but soon uncovered a trail of people — mostly women and children — who had gone missing after being seen in his company. Holmes was ultimately convicted of one murder, but suspected of killing at least 27 people and possibly as many as 200.

Public interest in serial killers waned until the 1970s and 1980s, when a succession of serial murders dominated the media and once again captivated readers. Son of Sam terrorized residents of New York City for a year by shooting unsuspecting couples in cars. The murders, along with letters from the killer warning of more to come, led to the largest manhunt in the city's history. John Wayne Gacy, however, quietly lured teenage boys and young men to his house in a suburb of Chicago, where he raped, murdered and buried them. Shock and horror came later, as photos of police officers carrying out body after body were published in newspapers around the country.

In the early 1990s, police were alerted by neighbors to loud noises, terrible smells and the presence of a disoriented, naked and bleeding teenage boy wandering the streets outside Jeffrey Dahmer's apartment in Milwaukee, Wis. A handsome man with an easy smile, Dahmer persuaded the officers that there was nothing amiss. Two months later, after a second intended victim escaped and reported the attempted murder, police came back, this time finding butchered body parts, an electric buzz saw and a 57-gallon drum filled with acid for dissolving unwanted bones.

Dennis L. Rader committed seven murders in Wichita, Kan., between 1974 and 1991. He gave himself the name B.T.K. — for his preferred method of binding, torturing and killing — in letters he sent to police, along with souvenirs taken from his victims. Wichita residents worried that the killer was one of them, and they were right: B.T.K. turned out to be a longtime neighbor, family man and church leader. But he wasn't caught until 2005, after he sent a letter and a copy of a victim's driver's license to the local newspaper.

California's Golden State Killer was perhaps the most violent of them all, committing scores of crimes ranging from burglary to rape to murder over a span of 10 years. Thirty years after the killer committed his last crime, former police officer Joseph DeAngelo was arrested after police matched DNA from a crime scene to relatives listed on a genealogy website.

Most serial killers have families, homes and jobs. They go to church, are Boy Scout troop leaders and serve in the military. They are relatives, neighbors and friends. They hide in plain sight.

CHAPTER 1

Jack the Ripper

The people of London had never seen anything like the mutilated bodies left by the serial killer Jack the Ripper. Targeting female prostitutes in London's impoverished Whitechapel district, the killer slit their throats, ripped open their torsos and mutilated their genitals and faces. News stories of the murders were so widely read that the legend of Jack the Ripper — as well as copycat murders — spread throughout Europe, Australia and the United States. As many as 100 men were arrested in connection with the murders, but none were convicted. The identity of Jack the Ripper remains a mystery.

Whitechapel's Mysterious Murderer.

BY THE NEW YORK TIMES | SEPT. 4, 1888

LONDON, SEPT. 3. — Whitechapel has a murder mystery which transcends anything known in the annals of the horrible. It is Poe's "Murders of the Rue Morgue" and "The Mystery of Marie Roget" rolled into one real story. It is nothing less than a midnight murderer, whose step is noiseless, whose strike is deadly, and whose cunning is so great that he leaves no trace whatever of his work and no clue to his identity. He has just slaughtered his third victim, and all the women in Whitechapel are terrified, while the stupidest detectives in the civilized world stand aghast and say they have no clue.

When the murder of Mary Ann Nichols, who was cut into ribbons last Friday night, was investigated it became evident that the murder was the work of the same hand that committed the two preceding ones.

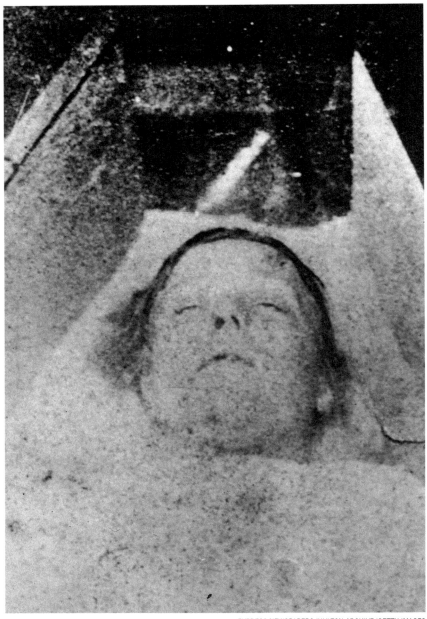

A mortuary photograph of Mary Ann Nichols.

All three were moneyless women of the lowest class. All were killed in the street between 1 and 3 o'clock in the morning, and all were mutilated in the same fiendish and peculiar way. The coincidence was so great as to strike even the detectives, and they are now looking for the one man whom they believe to be guilty of all three crimes.

This man is called "Leather Apron" and nobody knows him by any other name. He is in character half way between Dickens's Quilp and Poe's Baboon. He is short, stunted, and thick set. He has small, wicked black eyes and is half crazy. He is always hanging about the deep shadows that fill the intricate network of the courts, passages, and alleyways in Whitechapel. He does not walk, but always moves on a sharp, queer run and never makes any noise with his feet. In addition to the three women he is believed to have murdered he has scared a hundred more of them nearly to death. Every streetwalker in Whitechapel has her own story to tell of him. He lives by robbing them late at night and has kicked, cuffed, or knocked down two score of them in the last two years. His usual lodging place is a fourpenny lodging house in a poverty-stricken thieves' alley off Brick-lane. He has left there now, however, and nobody knows where he is.

He is suspected of having done the three murders from the fact that he has frequently drawn a knife on women, accompanied by the same threats which have been carried out on the dead women. The story of Mrs. Colwall, who heard the screams of the woman as she was being murdered, is to the effect that she was clearly running away from somebody who was murdering her, and yet she could hear no other footsteps. The blood stains on the sidewalk indicated the same thing — that the murderer, whoever he was, was noiseless in his pursuit, and this quality points directly to "Leather Apron." He is a slippermaker by trade, and gets his nickname from the fact that he always wears a leather apron and is never seen without it. One peculiar feature of the case is that none of the police or detectives appears to know him, he having always kept out of their sight, and they are now gleaning information concerning him from women he has assailed.

Whitechapel Startled by a Fourth Murder.

BY THE NEW YORK TIMES | SEPT. 8, 1888

LONDON, SEPT. 8. — Not even during the riots and fog of February 1886 have I seen London so thoroughly excited as it is to-night. The White-chapel fiend murdered his fourth victim this morning and still contin-ues undetected, unseen, and unknown. There is a panic in Whitechapel which will instantly extend to other districts should he change his locality, as the four murders are in everybody's mouth.

The papers are full of them, and nothing else is talked of. The latest murder is exactly like its predecessor. The victim was a woman street walker of the lowest class.

She had no money, having been refused lodgings shortly before because she lacked 8d. Her throat was cut so completely that every-thing but the spine was severed, and the body was ripped up, all the viscera being scattered about. The murder in all its details was inhu-man to the last degree, and, like the others, could have been the work only of a bloodthirsty beast in human shape. It was committed in the most daring manner possible. The victim was found in the back yard of a house in Hanbury-street at 6 o'clock. At 5:15 the yard was empty. To get there the murderer must have led her through a passageway in the house full of sleeping people, and murdered her within a few yards of several people sleeping by open windows.

To get away, covered with blood as he must have been, he had to go back through the passageway and into a street filled with early mar-ket people, Spitalfields being close by. Nevertheless, not a sound was heard and no trace of the murderer exists.

All day long Whitechapel has been wild with excitement. The four murders have been committed within a gunshot of each other, but the detectives have no clue. The London police and detective force is probably the stupidest in the world. The man called "Leather Apron," of whom I cabled you, is still at large. He is well known, but they have not been able to arrest him, and he will doubtless do another murder in a day or so. One clue discovered this morning by a reporter may develop into something. An hour and a half after the murder a man with bloody hands, torn shirt, and a wild look entered a public house half a mile from the scene of the murder. The police have a good description of him, and are trying to trace it. The assassin, however, is as cunning as he is daring. Both in this and in the last murder he took but a few minutes to murder his victim in a spot which had been examined but a quarter of an hour before. Both the character of the deed and the cool cunning alike exhibit the qualities of a monomaniac.

Such a series of murders has not been known in London for a hundred years There is a bare possibility that it may turn out to be something like a case of Jekyll and Hyde, as Joseph Taylor, a perfectly reliable man, who saw the suspected person this morning in a shabby dress, swears that he has seen the same man coming out of lodging house in Wilton-street very differently dressed. However that may be, the murders are certainly the most ghastly and mysterious known to English police history. What adds to the weird effect they exert on the London mind is the fact that they occur while everybody is talking about Mansfield's "Jekyll and Hyde" at the Lyceum.

Dismay in Whitechapel; Two More Murdered Women Found.

BY THE NEW YORK TIMES | OCT. 1, 1888

LONDON, SEPT. 30. — The Whitechapel fiend has again set that district and all London in a state of terror. He murdered not one woman but two last night, and seems bent on beating all previous records in his unheard-of crimes. His last night's victims were both murdered within an hour, and the second was disemboweled like her predecessors, a portion of her abdomen being missing as in the last case. He contented himself with cutting the throat of the other, doubtless because of interruption. Both women were street walkers of the lowest class, as before.

These crimes are all of the most daring character. The first woman was killed in the open roadway within a few feet of the main street, and though many people were within a few feet distance, no cry was heard. This was at midnight; before 1 o'clock the second victim was found, and she was so warm that the murder must have taken place but a few minutes before. This was in Mitre-square, which is but a few blocks distant from the Bank of England, in the very heart of the business quarter. The square is deserted at night, but is patrolled every half hour at least by the police.

These make six murders to the fiend's credit, all within a half-mile radius. People are terrified and are loud in their complaints of the police, who have done absolutely nothing. They confess themselves without a clue, and they devote their entire energies to preventing the press from getting at the facts. They deny to reporters a sight of the scene or bodies, and give them no information whatever. The assassin is evidently mocking the police in his barbarous work. He waited until the two preceding inquests were quite finished, and then murdered two more women. He has promised to murder 20 in all, and has every prospect of uninterrupted success.

The London Paranoiac.

BY THE NEW YORK TIMES | OCT. 8, 1888

THERE IS, of course, no question as regards the insanity of the White-chapel murderer.

In the time of the bitter vendettas of the Middle Ages, in savage border wars between the whites and Indians, and among the cannibalistic Polynesians, similar murders have been committed with equally cruel mutilation by men whose sanity could not be questioned.

But in this age and in the very center of modern civilization there could be no incentive to such horrible crimes in the breasts of sane men, however unruly their passions or revengeful their natures. In the series of murders committed by Maximilian in DeQuincey's remarkable story of "The Avenger," the incentives to the deeds, terrible as were the wrongs to his family and race, were scarcely adequate to such wholesale butchery. The story is improbable, and were it true, its hero would necessarily be considered a lunatic.

The motives of homicidal maniacs are very diverse, and often difficult of analysis. Sometimes it is a melancholy mother who destroys her children under the delusion that she saves them from some threatening disaster, or because a voice commands her to sacrifice them. Sometimes it is some moral imbecile who delights in torturing innocent people to death. Often it is the victim of alcohol who "runs amuck," stabbing right and left through a crowded thoroughfare. Frenzied outbursts of violence in acute maniacs and general paretics are by no means infrequent.

But there is a class of lunatics, formerly known as monomaniacs, but to whom now the term paranoiac is applied, which constitutes the most dangerous of all the insane classes. The word monomania has been discarded because it was misleading in its derivation. Although the insane man may have but one dominating delusion, there are often minor delusions, defective reason and judgment centering about the so-called imperative conception, so that he can scarcely be said to be insane on one solitary subject, as the word monomania would imply. Paranoia is a form of insanity which develops in a person who from birth has a defective mental organization. In paranoia the intellect maybe unimpaired; there may indeed be unusual intellectual capacity. John Brown, Benvenuto Cellini, Guiteau, King Ludwig of Bavaria, and many others, both notorious and famous, were undoubtedly paranoiacs. Society is full of them in every class, high and low, educated and ignorant, and they vary in their characters from the mildly eccentric individuals to the most troublesome "cranks." The popular term for a paranoiac is a "crank," a person, peculiar from birth in his speech and conduct. The great trouble is that most of them are so bright intellectually or so useful, and injure society in general so little by their presence that they cannot be incarcerated, although they may be a life-long affliction to their immediate friends and companions. Happily their homicidal tendencies are upon the whole developed rarely.

The motives of homicidal paranoiacs are also various. For instance, Duborgne, who, some years ago, stabbed a number of women in Fourteenth-street, had far other reasons for so doing than this Whitechapel murderer. The former had delusions of persecution and hallucinations of hearing. He fancied he heard people reviling him as he passed through the street. He heard them say, "There goes the wretch who is taking all the money out of the country."

The Whitechapel murderer is actuated by one of two motives. He kills to satisfy a religious fanaticism or because of a perverted sexual instinct, or there may be a combination of the two impulses. The fact that his victims have been selected from the lowest classes of immoral women in London certainly inclines one to the opinion that his desire is to immolate these creatures upon the altar of religion, his delusions being that they are the chief emissaries of the devil in the spread of evil. Under the fiendish penal code which he has established it seems necessary to kill and mutilate these poor creatures. If this be really his sole imperative idea, however, it will be the only example of its kind in history. The religious paranoiac is not so apt to concentrate his reforms upon one vice alone. He usually makes war upon universal evil, but by insane methods; he harangues audiences, announces himself as a prophet perhaps, is constantly quoting the Bible to his associates, and often incites rebellion and riot. John Thom, who caused the bloody Canterbury riots in 1833, is an example in point of a religious paranoiac.

The fact that women of this class are selected should not be taken too seriously. That he selects women is a more important point. That they should be of a base type is quite as likely to be due to the necessities of the case. They are the only women he can induce to follow him into dark corner in the dead of night.

When, on the other, hand, the motive is excited by perversion of the sexual instinct with cannibalistic or similar insane propensities, the crimes are limited to women and the lunatic is more secretive. Andreas Bichel murdered young girls, cut open their warm bodies, and ate their quivering flesh. The Westphalia murders, a few years ago, with most shocking mutilation of the bodies, of which more than twenty young women were the victims, are of similar origin. Only recently in Texas there was a series of butcheries of young women all perpetrated under circumstances so peculiar as to point to a homicidal lunatic as their author.

The remarkable cunning of the London paranoiac, his secretiveness, his ability to elude the vigilant officers of justice in one of the most crowded quarters of the globe, his careful selection of victims of one sex, the singular mutilation to which he subjects them, all indicate that he is actuated by motives partly religious perhaps, but more than likely for the devilish gratification of perverted sexual instincts, and at the same time demonstrate him to be one of the most daring and atrocious homicidal lunatics of which medical jurisprudence has any record.

The Whitechapel Crime; No Clue to the Perpetrator of the Latest Murder.

BY THE NEW YORK TIMES | JULY 18, 1889

LONDON, JULY 17. — The woman whose body was found in Castle-alley, in the Whitechapel district, last night was a middle-aged female of the disreputable class. Her throat had been cut to the spine. When the body was found it was lying on its back. The abdomen had been slashed in a horrible manner in several places. No part of the body was missing. Warm blood was flowing from the wounds when the body was found.

A policeman, who with the watchman of an adjacent warehouse must have been within a few yards of the spot when the crime was committed, heard no noise. Policemen have been placed at fixed points in Whitechapel since the murders of this character began there, and since the one preceding that of last night officers have been stationed at a point within a hundred yards of the scene of the last tragedy. An old clay pipe smeared with blood was found alongside the body. It is supposed by the police that this will furnish a clue to the murderer, although it may have belonged to the victim.

Several arrests of suspected persons have been made, but they were discharged from custody, there being no proof on which to hold them.

It is stated that a letter was received by the police officials before last night's murder in Whitechapel signed "Jack the Ripper," in which the writer said that he was "about to resume his work."

A Warning to Whitechapel.

BY THE NEW YORK TIMES | OCT. 2, 1890

LONDON, OCT. 1. — The police of the Whitechapel district have received a warning from "Jack the Ripper" that he is about to kill another woman. The handwriting of the letter is identical with that of the other letters which it has been the custom of the murderer to send to the police prior to the murder and mutilation of some poor creature in Whitechapel.

Jack the Ripper Again.

BY THE NEW YORK TIMES | FEB. 13, 1891

LONDON, FEB. 13. — A renewal of the "Jack the Ripper" scare terrorizes that quarter of the city where the performances of the mysterious murderer have heretofore been the cause of so much alarm.

At an early hour this morning the body of a young woman was discovered in the secluded locality in Chambers Street. She had been horribly gashed with a sharp instrument. Nothing is yet known as to who she is or who her murderer was. The woman's head had been severed almost entirely from her body, and it was a ghastly spectacle that met those who viewed the remains.

Detectives quickly began a search for the murderer.

CHAPTER 2

First American Serial Killer: H. H. Holmes

Herman W. Mudgett, better known by one of his many aliases, H. H. Holmes, is believed to be the first serial killer in the United States. An accomplished insurance swindler and con man, Holmes was convicted of killing one person, confessed to killing 27 and is believed by some to have murdered as many as 200 around the time of Chicago's World Fair at the end of the 19th century. Caught, convicted and hanged, Holmes's life and crimes have inspired numerous investigative works, novels and documentaries.

May Be Charged with Murder

BY THE NEW YORK TIMES | NOV. 19, 1894

PHILADELPHIA, NOV. 18. — H. H. Holmes, alias H. H. Howard, the man arrested in Boston charged with swindling the Fidelity Mutual Life Insurance Association of this city out of $10,000 by palming off a bogus corpse as the body of B. F. Pietzel, a policy holder of the company, will be brought here to-morrow and arraigned on the charge. The charge of swindling may not be the only one Holmes will have to answer, for the more serious crime of murder may be laid to him.

When the body of the supposed Pietzel was found in the room at 1316 Callowhill Street on Sept. 3 last it was stretched flat upon the floor and was perfectly rigid. The Coroner's physician claims that the body could not have been brought here in a trunk from another city, as confessed to by Holmes, for the reason that it was stiff, and a body once bent does not again become rigid. Furthermore, if it had been in the trunk it would have shown marks of where it had been doubled up, and no such marks were upon the body. The theory is advanced that the body found was really that of Pietzel and not of any one else.

As a basis for this theory it is argued that Pietzel and the other conspirators plotted to disfigure the former by burning his face with some chemical and then calling in a physician to prescribe for his injuries. A body was then to be procured and similarly disfigured as Pietzel's was, and then it was to be given out that the man had died of his injuries, and it was trusted that the attending physician would not discover the fraud and would give a certificate of death in accordance with the story told by the conspirators. It is supposed that Pietzel had his fellow conspirators administer chloroform to him, so that he would not feel the pain of the burns when they were inflicted, and that he either was given an overdose and died from the effects or was killed while unconscious by his treacherous friends.

Another theory in support of the belief of murder is that a man resembling Pietzel was decoyed to the room, chloroformed and killed, and his face disfigured so as to render identification more difficult. Another suspicious circumstance, as viewed by the detectives, is that Mrs. Pietzel was home on a visit about a month ago to her parents, in Illinois, and she said nothing about the death of her husband.

In the neighborhood of Thirteenth and Callowhill Streets nobody could be found to-day who remembered or knew anything about Pietzel.

Holmes Killed Pietzel

BY THE NEW YORK TIMES | JULY 18, 1895

PHILADELPHIA, JULY 17. — District Attorney Graham, it is said, has been put in possession of new evidence of a circumstantial kind against H. H. Holmes, suspected of the murder of B. F. Pietzel, and the latter's three children. Mr. Graham is running down every clue that may lead to the unearthing of Holmes's crimes, and is doing all he can to aid the Toronto authorities in their collection of evidence. So far no claim has been made for Holmes from Toronto.

District Attorney Graham this afternoon said that there was little chance of Holmes being taken to Toronto to be tried for the murder of the Pietzel girls. He has found evidence, he said, which leads to the conclusion that the body found in the Callowhill Street house, in this city, was Pietzel's and he is now preparing to try Holmes here on the charge of murdering Pietzel.

Detective Geyer, who unearthed the bodies of the Pietzel girls in Toronto, is in almost hourly communication with the District Attorney. District Attorney Graham this afternoon received a telegram from him dated Toronto, which said: "I am going to Detroit to look for Howard Pietzel." Holmes is believed to have murdered Howard in that city, and Geyer is going there to endeavor to discover the body.

When taken before the District Attorney, Holmes, after his long confinement in prison, looked wearied, but still maintained his unequalled nerve. He is said to have remarked, "Well, I guess I will have to swing for this," but quickly recovered himself, and spun several more fairy tales to Mr. Graham, all of which were set down as falsehoods. It was said that Holmes made a full confession, but this Lawyer Barlow denies. "Nothing new was elicited at the conference," said Mr. Barlow, "and while the statements of Holmes added nothing materially new to the case, we secured from him certain data that will aid us in continuing our investigation of the strange affair."

Two portraits of Herman Webster Mudgett (also known as H. H. Holmes).

District Attorney Graham this afternoon made a long statement, giving the history of his office with the Pietzel insurance fraud case. Mr. Graham says that after Holmes's conviction upon the charge of conspiracy, he made every effort to obtain information from him as to the whereabouts of the Pietzel children. After detailing at some length Holmes's statement to him, Mr. Graham said that Holmes asserted most positively that the woman Minnie Williams and the three children sailed from New-York for London. Holmes's statement was that Minnie Williams went to London and set up a massage establishment at 8 Veder or Vader Street in that city, and that she was otherwise known as Adele, Corelle, and Geraldine Wandel. By Holmes's direction Mr. Graham inserted a cipher personal in the columns of a New-York paper June 2 last. This cipher, when translated, requested Minnie Williams to bring the children back to this country at once. Mr. Graham placed no credence in the cipher, and his belief was fully borne out, as no answer to it has ever been made. Detective Geyer was then detailed upon the case, and the result of his investigations was the finding of the bodies of the two children in Toronto.

Mr. Graham says that Holmes has told so many lies that he has even deceived his own counsel, who is now abroad looking up Minnie Williams. In concluding his statement, Mr. Graham says it is his design to have Holmes tried for the murder of Pietzel, but if it appears that he will be more easily convicted in Toronto, he will allow him to be taken there.

Holmes's counsel presents a bold front in his client's behalf, and asserts that Holmes is perfectly willing to go to Toronto to stand trial there for the murder of the two children. Mr. Shoemaker, Holmes's counsel, asserts that the burden of the proof will rest entirely upon the prosecution, and that it will be unable to prove that the bodies are even those of the Pietzel children, or that Holmes is the man that rented the house in Toronto. Mr. Shoemaker takes the same position in regard to the murder charge against Holmes in this city. He says that the prosecution will be unable to prove that the body of the man found in the house on Callowhill Street was Pietzel's.

Thomas A. Fahy, counsel for Mrs. Pietzel, has received no word from her since the finding of her children's bodies. But from other sources it is learned that she is in deep distress over the news, and is nearly crazed with apprehension for the possible fate of her boy, Howard. At present she is in Chicago, at 6036 Sangamon Street, having left Galva, Ill., a week ago for the purpose of consulting an agent of the Fidelity Mutual Life Association in the hope of finding something of the whereabouts of her children. Her eldest daughter, Dessie, and the baby are at her parents' home in Galva. Mrs. Pietzel is broken in health, and it is feared that she may not be strong enough to survive the last shock. Mr. Fahy said that she would be present at the trial of Holmes for murder, whether it took place here or in Toronto.

The Williams Girls' Fate; Probably Murdered and Burned by Holmes at Chicago.

BY THE NEW YORK TIMES | JULY 21, 1895

CHICAGO, JULY 20. — New evidence of murder was brought to light this morning in the residence at 701 Sixty-third Street, formerly occupied by H. H. Holmes, the insurance swindler.

Detective Fitzpatrick was looking around the building this morning, when he discovered in an ash heap the charred remains of a woman's high French-heeled buttoned shoe, and also a piece of grosgrain silk, about five inches square. These bits of women's attire are supposed to have belonged to one of the Williams girls, but there was nothing on either by which it might have been identified.

The work of excavation will be continued under the direction of Inspector Fitzpatrick of the Central Detective Detail. When a thorough overhauling of the premises once occupied by Holmes has been made the house at Sixty-sixth and Halsted Streets will be systematically searched. This is the house in which Anna Williams dwelt for a while, and the officers expect to find there some substantial proof that she was murdered in her own residence. Holmes, it is said, divided his time about equally between this house and the one at Wallace and Sixty-third Streets, which is now under investigation.

All last night two detectives from the Central Station were engaged in digging in the basement of the building at 701 Sixty-third Street, in search of the bodies of Minnie Williams and her sister.

During the World's Fair Dr. Holmes occupied the lower floor of the building, and Minnie Williams and her sister lived with him. They were beautiful and possessed of considerable money. Suddenly the sisters disappeared. Nothing was thought of the matter at the time, as it was supposed that they had gone to friends in different parts of the country. The arrest of Holmes for the murder of Pietzel gave rise to the rumor that both the Williams sisters had been murdered by Holmes, and that their bodies had been buried in the cellar of the building occupied by Holmes. Detectives were put to work on the case at the time, and so strong was the suspicion that it was decided to excavate in the cellar for the remains of the missing sisters.

This, however, was objected to by the occupants of the first floor, and was abandoned. Since the finding of the bodies of the Pietzel children in Toronto, the mysterious disappearance of the William sisters while they were members of Dr. Holmes's household was recalled by the police, and yesterday Inspector Fitzpatrick determined upon a thorough investigation.

After two hours' digging in the cellar an old stove was discovered, and in the firebox was found a quantity of charred human bones and a watchchain, formerly owned and worn by Minnie Williams. The jeweler who sold the chain to the missing girl was found and fully identified the chain as a portion of one sold by him to Minnie Williams during the World's Fair, shortly before her disappearance.

Miss Minnie Williams was possessed of $2,000 in cash and an estate of $50,000. Her friends and detectives have searched every city in the United States, without finding any trace of her. Her fortune passed into the hands of Holmes, and from him to another man whose name is supposed to be only another name for Holmes himself. Miss Williams came from Fort Worth, Texas. She was still a minor when she came to Chicago, and, as she could not come into the possession of her property, she became a stenographer. She chose to continue in her work after her fortune had come into her hands. She was employed in a down-town law office, and there met Holmes.

Shortly after their meeting Holmes organized the Campbell-Yates Company, advertised to buy and sell anything, and Miss Williams became stenographer for the firm. Her sister Anna was on a visit to her when both disappeared.

Accused of Ten Murders

BY THE NEW YORK TIMES | JULY 26, 1895

CHICAGO, JULY 23. — It is regarded as a rather uneventful day in police circles when the name of H. H. Holmes is not connected with the mysterious disappearance of one or more persons who were last seen in his company. Detectives who are thoroughly conversant with the Holmes case now believe that the self-confessed insurance swindler has been guilty of at least ten murders, and name the following as his victims:

CIGRAND, MISS, *of Indiana, who was associated with Holmes for six months.*

CONNOR, — , *daughter of I. L. Connor.*

CONNOR. MRS. I. L., *who left her husband for Holmes.*

DURKY, KATE, *a girl whose life Holmes insured.*

PIETZEL, ALICE, *found murdered at Toronto.*

PIETZEL, B. F., *found dead in Philadelphia; for securing the insurance on Pietzel's life, on his confession that he had substituted a body for that of Pietzel, Holmes was convicted of fraud and is now awaiting sentence.*

PIETZEL, NETTIE, *found murdered at Toronto.*

PIETZEL, HOWARD, *last seen with Holmes at Indianapolis Oct. 21, 1894.*

QUINLAN, CORA, *aged eleven, daughter of Janitor Quinlan; Holmes had her life insured for $1,000.*

WILLIAMS, ANNIE, *Holmes's stenographer and mistress.*

WILLIAMS, MINNIE, *sister of Annie; Holmes says she was killed by Annie in a fit of jealousy and that he put her body in a trunk and sunk it in Lake Michigan.*

The names of Miss Cigrand, Cora Quinlan and Kate Durky have been added to the list of Holmes's supposed victims within the last forty-eight hours. Patrick Quinlan, a former janitor at the Holmes house, Sixty-third and Wallace Streets, was in the "sweat box" at Police Headquarters last night for several hours. Holmes, he said, first told him Mrs. Connor had gone to the North Side, to remain a few weeks, and he afterward said she had gone to California to live, and had got married there. Holmes had Quinlan's eleven-year-old daughter Cora insured for $1,000, but whether or not he had ever collected the insurance was not known. Quinlan says he can produce his daughter, if necessary. Quinlan made many contradictory and improbable statements, and the police believe he can be made to tell a great deal more than he has yet told.

Mrs. Quinlan, the wife of the janitor, was in the "sweat box" for three hours this morning. The police believe that Quinlan knows a great deal about Holmes's affairs, and that he has confided in his wife. On leaving Police Headquarters Quinlan was accompanied by a police officer, who would not permit her to speak to reporters.

Mrs. W. L. Doyle, a friend of Mrs. Quinlan, was next questioned for half an hour. Before her examination she stated to a reporter that a young lady named Cigrand, who lived with Holmes just before the Williams girl, and who came to Chicago from Indiana, had mysteriously disappeared.

To the police to-day Mrs. W. L. Doyle said that her aunt owned the house where the two Pietzel children were found dead. Mrs. Doyle was shown a picture of the Pietzel children and of the excavations in the basement of the Holmes "Castle" here, of which she said: "Those are much better pictures than were in the Toronto papers of the house there, and of the children."

Asked how she knew the pictures were better she said: "I had a paper sent to me from Toronto, and the pictures in it were horrible."

Mrs. Doyle was asked how the paper came to be sent to her, and what interest she had in the case. She replied: "Well, you see, it's funny, but my aunt owns the house that Holmes lived in in Toronto. She rented it to him."

"Do you mean the house where the bodies of the two Pietzel children were found?"

"Yes," she replied.

Mrs. Doyle was asked if she knew Pietzel, to which she hesitatingly replied that she had met him, but she refused to say anything further about her acquaintance with the man Holmes is supposed to have murdered.

Miss Cigrand lived with Holmes at Sixty-third and Wallace Streets just before he had the Williams girl there. The neighbors remember little of the girl — not even her first name. She was a stately looking blonde, about twenty-five years of age, and lived with Holmes something less than six months. When she went away Holmes told Jeweler Davis, as the latter claims, that he had succeeded in "marrying her off." This is very much like what he told concerning the disappearance of Mrs. Connor. He said at the time that he had married her off in California. Miss Cigrand came to Chicago from Indiana. She associated but little with the neighbors, and even the other inmates of the building were in complete ignorance concerning her habits. Holmes was not often seen with her, and on these occasions he kept aloof from his acquaintances and introduced her to no one. Mrs. Doyle knows more about this girl, it is believed, than anybody else, but the Central Station officers will not permit her to talk about the case.

A. L. Jones, the man who purchased the drug store from Holmes, is positive that Holmes is guilty of the crime attributed to him and insists that Holmes also ended the life of Kate Durky, a young woman who was for a time his practical slave. The girl had her life insured and helped Holmes in many of his shady undertakings.

"Holmes was digging in that cellar day and night, and I now think that he was burying the bodies of those he had slaughtered," said Jones.

The excavation of the cellar of the Sixty-third Street house was continued to-day. The remains of a furnace that was possibly used by

Holmes as a crematory were unearthed. The man who built it was on the spot early in the day and told the policeman on duty that Holmes maintained great secrecy concerning its construction, and said that it was to be used in his gas-manufacturing experiments. As no attempt was ever made to make gas, this story was clearly a fabrication. The furnace had an air-tight receptacle in which could be generated a heat of 2,400° Fahrenheit, and was just long enough to contain a body.

One of the workmen to-day found in a pile of rubbish a letter, signed "H. H. Howard," and dated May 5, 1895. The signature is one of the many aliases used by Holmes, and one of the commonest of the lot. The letter is in his well-known handwriting, and is addressed to an occupant of the building, to whom the detectives who took possession of the letter before the reporters could get hold of it refused to state. It is believed, however, that the letter was to C. E. Davis, the jeweler, who occupies the building with Druggist Robinson.

The letter inquires particularly as to the doings of Janitor Quinlan and asks where he now is. It then goes on in a jocular manner to discuss the fate of the Williams girls, and asks of the recipient whether he has seen them or their ghosts about the building. Special inquiry is made as to the partitions in the house, and, in conclusion, the writer expresses the belief that he will not have to stay in jail much longer.

A few more bones were found to-day in the same hold from which those were taken yesterday. They were vertebrae and a portion of a human shoulder blade.

It was thought this morning that the Holmes house would be pulled down, having been condemned, but P. R. Chandler, a broker, who holds a mortgage on it for $12,000, advanced to Holmes with which to build, was told by the Building Inspector that all that was necessary was to improve the upper portion. This will be done at once. An order of foreclosure has already been secured from the court, and to-morrow or next day an order will be asked for allowing the improvements to be put on. The property is now worth $40,000. Besides the principal there is $4,000 back interest and taxes due on it.

Two curiosity seekers broke into the storeroom in the house to-day. The two men ransacked the room, everything was turned upside down, and a portion of the contents carried away. Holmes's bank books and a stack of legal documents, however, were overlooked. One of the men, it is said, is preparing the manuscript for a book about the Holmes affair, and was searching for information. The belief is gaining ground that Holmes's wife, who lives at the suburb of Wilmette, knows much more of the crimes of her husband than she cares to tell. It is probable that she will be put in the "sweatbox."

A man who gave his name as Capps, and said he was an attorney from Texas, inquired at the County Clerk's office to-day if the records showed that Henry H. Holmes was a notary public. The list of notaries showed his name, and that he had qualified as such July 24, 1888. Attorney Capps wanted to find out if the signature of Holmes on the county Clerk's books was the same as one on a deed. Minnie Williams, according to Capp's story, had signed a deed in which she had appeared before Holmes, and which he had signed as a notary. After examining Holmes's signature in the records, Capps pronounced them the same. Capps refused to say for what purpose he wished the information.

Still Another Victim.

BY THE NEW YORK TIMES | JULY 29, 1895

AURORA, ILL., JULY 28. — Albert Phillips, father of Clarence Phillips, who conducted a restaurant in Holmes's building on Sixty-third Street during the World's Fair, is confident that Holmes is responsible for the disappearance of still another victim than those so far known. Her name was Mrs. Lee.

Albert Phillips for several months assisted his son Clarence in conducting his restaurant, and became well acquainted with Holmes during that time. He said to-day: "The revelations in the case of Holmes make clear to me the mystery of the disappearance of Mrs. Lee while I was at the restaurant. She went out of sight as completely and mysteriously as though she had fallen off the earth, and my son and I were greatly puzzled over it at the time. Mrs. Lee came to the place while I was there. She was a handsome brunette, tall and stately, and well dressed. She often displayed bank notes of large denominations, claimed to be worth $60,000, and said that her husband and two children had died two years before. I wondered why a woman of her means should be content with the accommodations of our place, and I finally made up my mind it was for the society of Holmes. I often spoke with her while serving her at the table, and found her agreeable and intelligent. One day she was missing. We never knew where or how she went.

"I studied Holmes well while at the restaurant, and knew him as a sleek, smooth rascal. I had evidence of his crooked business dealings daily, but did not then suspect he was steeped in crime. Pat Quinlan seemed to be his confidant in every undertaking."

Holmes Had Sharp Knives and Saws; They Were Sharpened Just Before Howard Pietzel Died.

BY THE NEW YORK TIMES | SEPT. 3, 1895

INDIANAPOLIS, IND., SEPT. 2. — Albert Schiffling, an expert instrument maker of this city, met H. H. Holmes Oct. 3, 1894. Holmes called at his place of business that day, with two cases of instruments. The cases were of brown morocco leather. One case contained two knives and a saw. The knives were quite sharp, pointed at the ends, and the blades bore a few dark spots. In shape they resembled ordinary carving knives. The saw was of very fine make, and fifteen inches in length. The other case was much smaller, and contained, according to Mr. Schiffling's recollection, eight knives, of various sizes and shapes.

Holmes asked Schiffling to sharpen all the knives, saying he would return for them the next day. With him on this occasion was the boy, Howard Pietzel, and a strange man with a beard. Holmes did not call the next day, but returned Oct. 8, and secured the instruments. On the last visit Howard Pietzel was again with Holmes, but the strange man was not. Holmes seemed to be in a hurry, paid for the work and left at once. These knives were doubtless used to dismember young Pietzel before his body was burned in the Irvington house.

The Case Opened.

BY THE NEW YORK TIMES | OCT. 29, 1895

PHILADELPHIA, OCT. 28. — The Holmes case was called shortly after 10 o'clock this morning. Holmes walked jauntily into the dock, a tipstaff on either side of him. He was rather pale from long confinement in the county prison, but his black beard was neatly trimmed and his black suit of clothing gave him a dressy appearance. He took his seat with a calmness that was noticeable, and while he evinced a decided interest in the matters at issue, there was no look of fear upon his countenance, nor any evidence of nervousness in his action.

After the formalities in connection with the opening of the court had been concluded, Attorney W. H. Shoemaker, of counsel for the prisoner, in an address of some length, asked for a postponement of the case for sixty days. Mr. Shoemaker's contention was that the defense was not prepared for trial; that no witnesses were present. District Attorney Graham strenuously opposed the motion, declaring that the States's witnesses were present of their own volition, and that if a continuance should be granted, it would mean "the absolute destruction of the Commonwealth's case." Mrs. Pietzel's health was impaired, Mr. Graham further said, and if the case should be postponed, the strain would intensify her illness.

Samuel P. Rotan, for the defense, then addressed the Court, and claimed that, as Holmes was charged with the highest crime on the calendar, and other cases were involved, it would be necessary to investigate the dependent cases before proceeding. The attorney pleaded for time in which he and his colleagues could realize on Holmes's assets, and thus bring witnesses to Philadelphia who will not come unless their expenses are paid. The discovery of new testimony within the last four or five days, which he wanted to investigate, was a further plea of the attorney for a continuance.

Judge Arnold overruled the motions for postponement in a very few words, and ordered the trial to go on. Judge Arnold stated that there would be no farce in court, but a trial, and again directed that the jury be called and the prisoner tried on the indictment.

The first talesman called to be examined was Enoch Turner, a conductor. District Attorney Graham said he desired to state to the juror, and ask the attention of other jurors at the same time to avoid the necessity of repetition, that the case about to be tried was that of the Commonwealth vs. Herman W. Mudgett, alias H. H. Holmes, charged with the murder of Benjamin F. Pietzel.

After asking the talesman several questions, the District Attorney turned him over to the defense, but Attorney Shoemaker, addressing Judge Arnold, said:

Will you allow this case to go over until tomorrow, in order to make what preparation we can with regard to it?

The Court — This case must go on.

At this point Attorney Rotan informed the Court that the prisoner wished to be heard, and Holmes, rising from his seat in the dock, addressing the Court, said:

May it please the Court, I have no inclination to ask the present counsel to continue in the case, where I can see it will be against their own interest. Bearing this fact in mind, I have within the last few moments discharged them from the case.

The Court — They cannot be discharged from the case, and if they leave the court they will be punished as lawyers are punished for disobedience.

Mr. Rotan — We do not ask to leave the court or to leave the case; but we desire, as we said some time ago, to have further time, and now, rather than go on with the case, we ask to withdraw.

The Court — Gentlemen, as I said before, your application to withdraw is refused.

Holmes — If the Court please, if I can have a continuance even for one day, I feel sure —

The Court — That has been refused already. We can go on with the business to-day, and keep the case running for a day or two.

Holmes — Will not the case be allowed to go over for a day when I state to the Court that I can get another lawyer to attend to my interests?

The Court — You will have time to-morrow to get another lawyer, but the case must go on today.

Mr. Rotan — The prisoner stated that he intends to examine these jurors, and it is not interfering with the counsel. He says he is going to attend to the examination of these jurors.

The Court — Let him examine them, then.

Mr. Shoemaker — He might be able to get other counsel for to-morrow, but we are not able to go on with this case.

The Court — We will occupy the day as much as we can, Mr. Shoemaker. We cannot get through with the case to-day, and you will have an opportunity to get other counsel by to-morrow morning. Go on and occupy to-day, and get on as far as you can. Will you examine the witness?

HOLMES EXAMINES JURORS.

Holmes, in response to this query, proceeded to examine the juror, and finally asked that the juror be discharged peremptorily. The challenge was overruled.

The next juror called was Frederick Schlump, Sr. He was found to be unobjectionable by the Commonwealth, and was examined by Holmes in person, and at the end of that examination was permitted to take a seat in the box.

At the end of this examination Mr. Rotan addressed the Court, saying:

May it please your Honor, the prisoner won't let me do anything, and I will have to retire from the court.

Judge Arnold — I advise you not to do it.

Mr. Rotan — With all respect to the Court, I fear that I will have to do it. He says he won't allow me to do anything. It is useless, therefore, for me to remain, and I will have to withdraw. I do not understand my position. After having stated to the Court our purpose to withdraw, and having heard the Court's opinion upon that purpose, we are told by the prisoner that he won't let us do anything for him. I do it reluctantly, but under the circumstances I will have to withdraw. I believe that I am doing my duty.

Judge Arnold — Very well, you will both have to bear the consequences. You know what they are.

Both Mr. Rotan and Mr. Shoemaker then withdrew from the court without saying a word to the prisoner.

Mr. Graham then called Everett A. Schofield to the bar of the court, and another young attorney, and after a conversation with Judge Arnold, Mr. Graham moved the Court for the appointment of counsel to protect the defendant's rights. Judge Arnold was about to assign them, and they had taken their seats at the attorney's table, when Holmes arose, and, addressing the Court, said:

> To have an attorney thrust upon me at this time, and one who is not at all familiar with the case, were I to permit him to represent me, would be, in my opinion, to sacrifice my life. I had intended, after the adjournment of the case to-day to ask for leave to consult with a party with whom money had been placed so that I could consult with Mr. R. O. Moon, who has some knowledge of the case, and engage his services. I feel that I am able to look after my own interests for this day.

Judge Arnold — Then you refuse the assignment of counsel?

Holmes — I must refuse, with the request that I may be permitted to consult after the adjournment of the court to-day with the persons I have mentioned.

Judge Arnold — The case will go on. You can examine the jurors yourself, and you can have the consultation to-night.

The calling of jurors was then resumed, and after several had been called and examined, Holmes, addressing Judge Arnold, said:

Holmes — Can I sit at the desk so as to be nearer the jurors and the Court?

Judge Arnold — That can't be done.

Holmes — My voice has not been used much for a year; it is weak, and I fear if it is used much it may get weaker, and if I were nearer the Court and jury I could be heard better.

Judge Arnold — Though your voice is weak, we can hear you; the court is very quiet.

Holmes — If I should after to-day go on without counsel, could the dock be placed nearer the rail?

Judge Arnold — We will think of that hereafter.

When Richard Johnson was called, the District Attorney asked him whether he had read or discussed a sensational book published by the defendant, entitled "Holmes's Own Story."

"This is not the time or place to discuss that question," interrupted Holmes, "I have published no book, or authorized any to be published."

"I know better," said Mr. Graham.

The juror answered "No" to the question, however, whereupon he was accepted without further discussion.

MOON WILL NOT SERVE.

At this stage of the proceedings Attorney R. O. Moon entered the courtroom, and when the Court was so informed a few moments' delay was allowed while Mr. Moon conversed with the prisoner. At the conclusion of their conference, Mr. Moon, addressing Judge Arnold, said:

> In response to the request of the prisoner, I have come up here, and after a brief consultation with him I would say that, of course, it is impossible for me to take charge of this case. I, perhaps, know as much as any counsel could know about the case, and I would say that practically I have not been consulted in this matter, although efforts have been made to retain me, but, for reasons, I have not accepted a retainer.
>
> I have declined to take part in the case, and the position in which I find myself now, no matter how earnestly I might desire to aid this man in the preparation of the case, which covers affairs and transactions which I have not had the opportunity to examine or investigate at all — no matter how earnestly I might desire to serve the prisoner, or however willing I might be to lay aside my own professional engagements, I feel, that, in the absence of preparation, I should be utterly powerless to aid the prisoner. Therefore I must decline, and I am frank to say so to the Court.

Judge Arnold — The prisoner has exercised his right in choosing counsel, and has taken charge of his own case.

The calling of jurors was again resumed. Juror Michael J. Scanlon was severely cross-examined by Holmes, who finally challenged him peremptorily. Holmes then challenged John McLaughlin and John C. Risley, peremptorily, and asked the Court if he had a right to make further challenges.

"Yes, up to the time the jury is sworn," said Mr. Graham.

"I would rather have my instruction from the Court than from you, Mr. Graham," coolly replied Holmes.

John Richardson, Sr., weaver, was then called, and his answers proved satisfactory to the District Attorney. He was, however, peremptorily challenged by Holmes.

When the box had been filled for the second time, Mr. Graham instructed the crier to ask the prisoner if he was satisfied, and if he was, to swear the jury. Holmes, without waiting for the question of the crier, asked the Court whether the District Attorney had the right to further challenge jurors, if he, Holmes, were not to exercise that right. Judge Arnold replied that the District Attorney could challenge until the jury was sworn. Holmes then peremptorily set aside Shreve, Ackley, and Charles Wasson.

After exercising his right to challenge peremptorily, and the box having been filled by jurors subsequently called, Holmes inquired how many challenges he had made, and was told sixteen, leaving him four more. He then addressed Judge Arnold, saying:

I urgently ask that the case be continued until to-morrow morning, before I decide whether I shall elect to make any further challenges, and so that I can have the consultation I desire, and an opportunity to send to Mr. Rotan for papers in possession of my former counsel.

Judge Arnold — I will send for the papers, but the case must go on.

Holmes — The delay is but short, and I feel that If I were given this day I should be able to get counsel.

Judge Arnold — You have discharged your counsel, and the case must go on. We cannot lock up the jury all night to oblige you.

Holmes pressed for the delay, and said that, so far as he was concerned, he did not care about having the jury locked up.

District Attorney Graham — It is the law.

Judge Arnold — You have discharged your counsel, and the case has been called and we intend that it shall go straight on. There must be no motion for a delay. (To the Clerk of the court) — Swear the jury.

Holmes — I desire to challenge two, if that is the last resort.

A JURY SECURED.

He was permitted to do so, and within a few minutes thereafter, the box being again filled, both the Commonwealth and the prisoner expressed satisfaction with it. Clerk Henszey then swore the jury severally, and recited the indictment charging Holmes with the murder of Benjamin F. Pietzel, and instructed them as to their duties. This being done, the court took a recess until 3 o'clock. Following are the names of the jurors selected; William P. Hansel, blacksmith; Linford Biles, paymaster; Robert Chambers, carter; George V. Clash, soapmaker; Louis Reese, farmer; Thomas Sloan, driver; John J. Smith, engineer; Andrew Hertel, shoemaker; Richard Johnson, painter; James Kenny, foreman; Robert J. Kinkaid, florist; Samuel Wood, manufacturer. The trial was resumed at 3:30 o'clock, and nearly all of the session, which continued until 4:55 o'clock, was taken up by District Attorney Graham in outlining the case to the jury.

The opening address of the District Attorney was forcible throughout, but his denunciations of Holmes, which were at times particularly severe, had no outward effect upon the accused. Holmes's composure was wonderful, and during the narrative he busied himself in taking copious notes of the prosecuting officer's address.

Mr. Graham at the outset stated that under the indictment, and providing the evidence should warrant it, it would be possible for the jury to find a verdict either of manslaughter, of murder in the second degree, of murder in the first degree, or of acquittal. He declared, however, that he would ask for a verdict of first degree murder.

The District Attorney went into the story of Benjamin F. Pietzel's death and the incidents connected therewith at great length. He told of the finding, Sept. 4, 1894, of a partly decomposed and mutilated body in the house 1318 Callowhill Street, in this city, which was supposed to be the body of "B. F. Perry," and who, it was believed, had been killed by an accidental explosion of chemicals; narrated the subsequent sending of a letter to the Fidelity Mutual Life Association of Philadelphia by Jeptha D. Howe, a St. Louis attorney, in which he stated that the body found in the Callowhill Street house was not that of a man named "Perry," but was in reality that of Benjamin F. Pietzel, and demanding, on behalf of his (Pietzel's) widow, the $10,000 insurance which Pietzel had upon his life; and followed up the burial of the body in Potter's Field, its exhumation by the insurance company, and its identification as Pietzel's body by Alice Pietzel, a daughter, and by Holmes.

Mr. Graham graphically pictured the many features of the case, and laid especial stress upon the work of Detective Frank Geyer in finding the charred remains of the children, Alice and Nellie Pietzel, in Toronto; of the discovery of the remains of the boy Howard Pietzel, at Irvington, Ind., and of the suspicion that the three children were victims of the accused.

THE COMMONWEALTH'S CASE.

During the course of his recital of the murder of Pietzel, Mr. Graham indicated that the Commonwealth expected to prove that Pietzel was chloroformed to death while drunk. Returning to the finding of the body in Philadelphia, the District Attorney pointed his finger at the prisoner and dramatically declared: "There is the man who murdered Pietzel. It was he who arranged the household effects, and, being a physician, he burned the body as to give it the appearance of having been killed by an explosion."

Holmes did not wince under this. Mr. Graham told of the conspiracy against the Fidelity Mutual Life Association; of the collection of $10,000 insurance therefrom on Pietzel's wife, minus about $285 which the company withheld for expenses, and of Mrs. Pietzel securing but $500 of the sum, $2,500 having been paid to Lawyer Howe and the balance having been secured by Holmes.

The opening address covered about every phase of this interesting case, and the District Attorney occupied an hour and a half in its delivery. He concluded by expressing a belief that the prisoner would be convicted as indicted.

The Court ordered an adjournment at the conclusion of the address, but before this was announced by the crier Holmes arose from his seat in the dock and asked Judge Arnold to instruct the prison authorities to place him in a lighted cell and have him supplied with writing material. The Judge replied that this would be attended to. Holmes's purpose is evidently to work far into the night on his own case. The accused also asked if he could send to Fort Worth, Texas, for certain papers. "A witness by the name of Samuels," Holmes continued, "is coming here to identify a note. If Samuels has not got two notes for $16,000, I would ask that he get them."

The District Attorney then stated that he had the notes in question, and would produce them. Holmes next requested that he be given a list of all the witnesses subpoenaed in the case, but Mr. Graham refused to accede to this. A request for copies of the conspiracy and murder indictments found against him met with better success, the Judge directing that they be given to the prisoner.

A TILT WITH THE PROSECUTOR.

The finale of the day's proceedings was in the form of a tilt between Holmes and the District Attorney. Holmes said that he desired to have an interview with his wife, whereupon Mr. Graham, who had referred to Holmes's alleged bigamy in his opening address, replied: "Which wife do you mean?"

"I mean," retorted the prisoner, "the lady whom you designated as Miss Yohe, and, by so doing, you cast a slur upon her, as upon myself."

Holmes augmented this with a statement that "Miss Yohe" was his legal wife.

Mr. Graham told Holmes that the lady did not want to see him; that she had told him so in his (Graham's) presence.

The accused declared that the District Attorney had intercepted his wife's communications to him, but this Mr. Graham denied, and the Court coincided with the prosecuting officer. Finally, Holmes asked that a note be sent to his wife, and a reply received, which "shall not be seen by the District Attorney." The Court granted his request. Holmes wanted to have a messenger other than a court attaché deliver the missive, but Judge Arnold stated that a sworn court attaché was eminently trustworthy.

The court adjourned until 10 A. M. tomorrow. Beginning to-morrow and continuing to the conclusion of the case, the court will hold three sessions daily, in the morning, afternoon, and night. This will be done in order to finish the case as early as possible. It is believed that the fate of Holmes will be in the jury's hands in about a week.

Judge Arnold stated after the adjournment that he would not press the case for disbarment against Messrs. Shoemaker and Rotan, in view of the fact that Holmes had refused counsel, and would conduct his own case.

Holmes Is Found Guilty

BY THE NEW YORK TIMES | NOV. 3, 1895

PHILADEPHIA, NOV. 2. — Herman W. Mudgett, or, as he is better known, H. H. Holmes, was to-night convicted of murder in the first degree for killing Benjamin F. Pietzel in this city Sept. 2, 1894. The jury needed but one ballot to reach this decision.

The jury retired at 5:45, at the conclusion of Judge Arnold's charge. After the retirement of the jury from the courtroom the spectators streamed out into the corridors and eagerly discussed what the verdict would probably be. There was considerable difference of opinion, as many believed the Commonwealth had not thoroughly established its case against Holmes, but the majority were inclined to believe that the jury would convict.

Word was sent to Judge Arnold at 8:35 that the jury was ready to give its verdict. When Judge Arnold entered the room there were not nearly as many people present as had attended the day session. The prisoner was brought in and placed in the dock. He was as impassive as ever, as he took his seat. The jury came in and took their places, and it needed but little skill as a mind reader to know what the word would be that the foreman would pronounce.

The Court ordered Holmes to arise and then, in reply to the question of the Court, the foreman of the jury pronounced the fatal words, "Guilty of murder in the first degree."

The verdict was greeted with absolute silence. The charge of the Judge must have foreshadowed what his fate would be but the word "Guilty" fell upon Holmes with stunning force. He made no outcry and exhibited no emotion of any kind — the blow was too stunning for noisy outbreaks. He sat down, and while the jury was polled each man answered to his name, and as each pronounced his sentence Holmes stared vacantly before him. His face looked like that of a corpse. It was as absolutely expressionless as a mask. Only a nervous twitching of the eyelids and the contraction and dilation of the eyes showed that it was a living, breathing man that sat in the dock.

Holmes slowly recovered. He realized that his counsel was making a motion for a new trial. His under lip fell and he ran his tongue across it, moistening the dryness, and, clasping his hands together, he leaned forward to listen to the Judge's decision. When Judge Arnold said that he would hear the application for a new trial Monday, Nov. 18, an expression of something like hope broke across Holmes's dull face. Turning to the court officers, he said in an eager whisper, "Monday, Nov. 18?" These were the only words he uttered.

Judge Arnold then expressed to Mr. Rotan and Mr. Shoemaker his appreciation of how difficult their task had been, and he complimented them that they had been able to make as good a show for the defense as they did. He intimated that their withdrawal from the case was a device of the prisoner.

In a manly, honest way Mr. Rotan gave the Court to understand that their withdrawal was no device of their own, but was done from a sincere conviction, because they believed they had not been given time to prepare their case.

Judge Arnold then ordered the prisoner removed. By this time Holmes had recovered much of his composure, and he walked from the room with the quick springy step that is natural to him. The Judge thanked the jury for their attention, and discharged them.

If ever a good name would have been a shield and buckler to a man in his hour of peril, that man is Holmes. If ever a man's black deeds rose up to confront and convict him, that man is Holmes. If Holmes had only been in the dock for the murder of Pietzel it is an open question if the prosecution would not have failed of conviction, but unquestionably his bloody record served to condemn him. The jury was never in doubt. When they retired from the court room they took their suppers, and then a brief discussion was had. One ballot was taken, and every man voted to convict. They consumed three hours for their retirement, from the courtroom, but they could have found a verdict in fifteen minutes if they had so wished.

The day was a trying one for Holmes. When he was brought into court this morning he showed that the strain was beginning to tell upon him. His manner showed that he was extremely nervous, but he did his best to conceal it. All through the long day, while Mr. Graham was making his closing argument, and his attorney was making his defense to the jury, he endeavored to relieve the tension of his mind by making hurried notes of the speakers's words.

Holmes appeared a trifle nervous when brought into court this morning, though he was cheerful. Mr. Shoemaker of counsel for the defense was ill and unable to be present. It was decided that only District Attorney Graham and Mr. Rotan should address the jury. Mr. Graham reviewed the evidence at considerable length, maintaining that it had established the Commonwealth's case in every detail. He insisted that the theory of Pietzel's suicide was wholly untenable.

Mr. Graham spoke for nearly three hours. Holmes listened intently, and made voluminous notes of Mr. Graham's words.

Holmes's pale face wore a more serious expression than it had yet borne when he came into court this afternoon, and as soon as he got into the dock he began to scan his notes. He paid no attention to the great crowd, and seemed utterly oblivious of the hundreds of eyes focused upon him. He consulted with Mr. Rotan when the latter came in, and as he talked he laid his hand in an appealing sort of way on his lawyer's arm. Mr. Rotan began his argument at 2:30 o'clock. He said:

"Let us look at what the Commonwealth has done. Most of the evidence relates to the identity of Mr. Pietzel. We do not dispute that this was Pietzel's body. That is the least point of the case. We acknowledge that the defendant and Pietzel had a number of schemes to swindle. They even had another scheme besides this one. Briefly, the Commonwealth's evidence shows this: That Holmes and Pietzel came to this city together under false names, and that Mrs. Howard was with them. It is also true that Mr. Holmes did take Mrs. Pietzel around the country.

We made no defense because we were satisfied that the Commonwealth did not make out its case, and that the evidence is more consistent with the theory of suicide than of murder. The facts are these: Sunday morning, Sept. 2, Mr. Holmes went to the house 1316 Callowhill Street. He found there the body on the third floor. Pietzel had committed suicide. We claim that Pietzel committed suicide by swallowing chloroform drawn through a quill. The Commonwealth claims that it is impossible that the body could have been taken down stairs, and that it could have been so arranged as it was found after rigor mortis had set in.

Has the Commonwealth shown how soon Holmes found this body after death? No. Is there any evidence to show that the defendant secured this insurance policy on the life of Pietzel? You may be sure not, or it would have been here. If the motive in the killing was to secure the money, why did not Holmes get Pietzel to have the policy made payable to him, instead of to Mrs. Pietzel? When Pietzel started for Philadelphia, he told his family not to be alarmed if he was reported dead. Up to that Saturday before the killing it has been testified that Pietzel was perfectly sober and well. The Commonwealth has put in evidence tending to show that Pietzel was drunk, and so was easily overpowered and killed by the defendant. The Commonwealth's own doctors testified that there was no evidence in the brain or stomach of Pietzel that he had been drunk before he was killed.

We cannot imagine that this slight, delicate man, effeminate in his habits, could have killed this strong, powerful man. There is no evidence that Pietzel was drunk. Holmes never left his house until 10:30 Sunday morning. Is it likely that Pietzel would have been asleep at that hour? The facts in the case warrant you, gentlemen, in supposing Holmes was only going to make a short call on Pietzel. Important and vital testimony was given by Mrs. Howard about their plans for going away."

Mr. Rotan read the testimony of Miss Yoke in relation to how Holmes had told her previously to Sunday that they would probably leave that day, and how she had half packed the trunk when he returned to the house. After reading the testimony Mr. Rotan continued:

"Now, gentlemen, why do you suppose this trunk was packed by Mrs. Howard if she did not expect to leave?"

Mr. Graham interrupted Mr. Rotan by saying:

"I think it only fair to say that Pietzel called on Holmes the Saturday night before. He told Miss Yoke that he was a man from the Pennsylvania Railroad, and the exact date of their leaving was not fixed until Holmes returned from his visit to Pietzel's house."

Resuming, Mr. Rotan said:

"We cannot assume that Holmes started out with the intention of killing Pietzel, for how could he know that he would be drunk or asleep, or in any condition so that he could overpower him? He was only following an original intention when he went away Sunday. They argue especially upon the testimony of Dr. Leffman, one of the greatest specialists in the country, that it would be impossible for a man to kill himself with chloroform and retain this position. This we do not deny. Take Mr. Holmes's statement made a year ago. Then he had no knowledge of the case of the Commonwealth. In the statement he says that was the body of Pietzel. He did not think that they would dare bring a charge of murder against him. There is no testimony which says that Mr. Pietzel did not kill himself except from the position of his body."

When Mr. Rotan had concluded, Judge Arnold charged the jury. He explained the various grades of murder, and particularly premeditated murder. He advised the jury that in the case before it there could be only be one grade of murder to consider, and that was murder in the first degree. He told the jury that the evidence in this case was entirely circumstantial, but that was not unusual, as many murder cases are decided by circumstantial evidence. In the present case there were three points to consider: First, is Benjamin F. Pietzel dead? Second, if dead, did he die a violent death? Third, If he died a violent death, did he commit suicide, or did the defendant kill him?

The Judge then reviewed the evidence. When that part of the doctor's testimony was reached in which it was stated that Pietzel had been killed by poison, and that it could not have been self-administered, Judge Arnold queried: "If the poison was not self-administered, then the question is, who did administer it to him?" Holmes shrank a little in his chair as he heard this ominous query.

In referring to Mrs. Pietzel's story, Judge Arnold said that it proved the truth of the old saying, "truth is stranger than fiction." He also said that if the woman's story was true, it was the most wonderful exhibition of the power of mind over mind that he had ever seen, and was stranger than any novel he had ever read.

For the motive for the crime, if the jury believed Mrs. Pietzel's story, it was to be found in the desire to obtain the insurance money from her.

Judge Arnold said that the jury could judge from the cross-examination of Miss Yoke relative to Holmes's departure on Sunday afternoon whether it was what is known in law as a flight.

Finishing his review of the evidence, Judge Arnold said that the adoption of suicide as a plea of defense was no uncommon one in trials.

The Judge also read certain law points submitted by the defense. One of these was that there was reasonable doubt that Pietzel was killed. On coming to this, the Judge stated that he refused this, as there was no reasonable doubt that Pietzel was killed.

The Judge's charge was, on the whole, unfavorable to the prisoner. Holmes listened quietly to it, but he seemed nervous. The Judge concluded his charge at 5:45, and the jury retired.

Holmes Cool to the End

BY THE NEW YORK TIMES | MAY 7, 1896

PHILADELPHIA, MAY 7. — Murderer Herman Mudgett, alias H. H. Holmes, was hanged, this morning in the County Prison for the killing of Benjamin F. Pietzel. The drop fell at 10:12 o'clock, and twenty minutes later he was pronounced dead.

Holmes was calm to the end, even to the extent of giving a word of advice to Assistant Superintendent Richardson as the latter was arranging the final details. He died as he had lived — unconcerned and thoughtless apparently of the future. Even, with the recollection still vividly before him of the recent confession, in which he admitted the killing of a score of persons of both sexes, and in all parts of the country, he denied everything, and almost his last words were a point-blank denial of any crimes committed except the deaths of two women at his hands by malpractice. In the murder of the several members of the Pietzel family, he denied all complicity, particularly of the father, for whose death, he stated he was suffering the penalty. Then, with the prayer of the spiritual attendants still sounding in his ears and a few low-spoken words to those about him, the trap was sprung, and beyond a few incidental post-mortem details the execution which terminated one of the worst criminal stories known to criminology was ended.

While the exact time of the execution was as usual, unannounced, it was generally supposed that the hour would be about 10 o'clock. Two hours before that time, however, those who were to attend began arriving, but admission to the prison was denied every one except those officials in direct touch with the institution until 9 o'clock. The gates were then opened, and the fourscore or more having tickets pressed into the inner court. Sheriff Clements had preceded the crowd, and was awaiting the arrival of those comprising his jury, that they might be sworn.

The jury comprised six physicians and a like number from other walks in life, all prominent in their respective stations. They were ex-Sheriff William H. Wright, Dr. Benjamin Pennebacker, John J. Ridgway, Councilman R. R. Bringhurst, Samuel L. Wood, Dr. W. Joseph Hearn, Dr. W. J. Roe, A. B. Detwiler, Dr. M. B. Dwight, Dr. J. C. Guernsey, James Hand, and Dr. John L. Phillips. In response to the calling of their names they ranged about the desk behind which stood Sheriff Clements, and then solemnly swore "to witness the execution of Herman W. Mudgett, alias H. H. Holmes, and certify the time and manner of such execution according to law."

Mr. Wood, one of the Sheriff's jury, was also a member of the jury that convicted Holmes.

Many prominent men were in attendance, some being from other cities, notable among whom were Dr. MacDonald of Washington, the famous criminologist; Sheriff S. R. Mason of Baltimore, Profs. W. Easterly Ashton and Ernest Laplace of the Medico-Chirurgical College; Dr. John S. Miller of St. Josephs's Hospital; Detective Frank Geyer, who conducted the case; President Fous and Solicitor Campbell of the Fidelity Mutual Life Insurance Company; Dr. J. Howard Taylor, representing the medical staff, Captain of Detectives Miller, and Lawyer Rotan, who conducted the defense of Holmes during the trial.

Mr. Rotan was early at the prison, but had been preceded by the Rev. Father Dailey and the Rev. Father MacPake, who administered the last rites of the church to the condemned man. They arrived shortly after 6 o'clock, and only a few minutes after Holmes had arisen. They remained with him last evening until 10:30 o'clock. The death watch was then being kept by Keeper George Weaver, who remained until relieved at 7 o'clock this morning by Keeper Henry. Weaver said this morning that Holmes had retired about midnight and slept soundly during the entire time until called at 6 o'clock. So sound were his slumbers in fact that twice was he called before awakening when the arrival of the Rev. Fathers Dailey and MacPake was announced. He greeted them warmly, but with the same air of self-possession that has marked his conduct throughout the entire case. They were come to administer the sacrament of communion, and every possible facility for privacy was extended by Superintendent Perkins of the prison. For nearly two hours they remained in the cell, and then were almost immediately succeeded by Lawyer Rotan, the legal adviser of Holmes.

While they were talking breakfast was served, and Holmes seemed to heartily enjoy the meal. It was substantial, but plain, consisting of eggs, toast, and coffee, which were taken with an evident relish. "He enjoyed it more than I could, even though only his attorney," remarked Mr. Rotan, after leaving the cell. "He is the most cool and possessed of all in any way connected with the case."

The remark seemed in no wise exaggerated. Every story was to the same effect, and to the end he maintained the same stoicism. It was not the blustering braggadocio of the bully or desperado, but the calm demeanor and quiet bearing that are compelled by a will of iron.

When the morning meal was ended and shortly before 9 o'clock, Holmes prepared to dress himself. Contrary to the general custom, he refused to don a new suit, but arrayed himself in trousers, vest, and cutaway coat of some dark mixed goods, of a pepper-and-salt effect, that had been worn by him frequently before. Even in this he was careful, giving every attention to even the most minute details of his toilet. Collar and necktie were, of course, not worn, but their place was taken by a white handkerchief knotted carelessly about the neck.

Ten o'clock had just sounded when a call came from the cell corridor for Sheriff Clements. He had been gone but a moment when the doors leading through the long corridors in which was placed the gallows were opened, and two by two, led by the Sheriff's jury, the party passed down. The gallows was about half way down the corridor, and to either side was a high partition that, once through the doors, shut off any view of the approach of the condemned as he came to the scaffold. Affairs were quickly approaching a crisis and the other incidents of the execution seemed to take shape and pass away with lightning-like rapidity. The last man of those attending had just passed through the doors and the latter closed, when from beyond was heard the slow and measured tread of the little coterie comprising the death party.

The greatest stillness prevailed among the group watching for the first glimpse of the condemned. Preceded by Sheriff Clements and Superintendent Perkins, Holmes soon stepped on to the trap. On the right was Father Dailey, to the left Father MacPake, and bringing up the rear were Lawyer Rotan and Assistant Superintendent Richardson. The little party stood for a moment looking down, and then in response to a sign from one of those beside him Holmes stepped forward and spoke. Pallid, naturally, after his incarceration, there was no other evidence of any fear or disquiet. He spoke slowly and with measured attention to every word; a trifle low at first, but louder as he proceeded, until every world was distinctly audible.

"Gentlemen," he said, "I have a very few words to say. In fact, I would make no statement at this time except that by not speaking I would appear to acquiesce in life in my execution. I only want to say that the extent of my wrongdoings in taking human life consisted in the deaths of two women, they having died at my hands as the result of criminal operations. I wish also state, however, so that there will be no misunderstanding hereafter, I am not guilty of taking the life of any of the Pietzel family, the three children or father, Benjamin F. Pietzel, of whose death I am now convicted and for which I am to-day to be hanged. That is all."

As he ceased speaking he stepped back, and, kneeling between Fathers Dailey and MacPake, joined with them in silent prayer for a minute or two. Again standing, he shook the hands of those about him, and then signified his readiness for the end.

Coolest of the entire party, he even went to the extreme of suggesting to the Assistant Superintendent Richardson, that the latter not hurry himself. "Take your time; don't bungle it," he remarked, as the official exhibited some little haste, the evident outcome of nervousness. Those were his last words. The cap was adjusted, a low-toned query: "Are you ready?" and an equally low-toned response, "Yes, good-bye," and the trap was sprung.

The neck was not broken, and there were a few convulsive twitches of the limbs that continued for about ten minutes. "But he suffered none after the drop," said Dr. Scott, the prison physician. The trap was sprung at precisely 10:12 ½ and fifteen minutes later Holmes was pronounced dead, though the body was not cut down until 10:45.

The body was placed in a vault in Holy Cross Cemetery. The last act in the vault was performed at Holmes's express command. The lid of the coffin was taken off and the body was lifted out and laid on the ground. Then the bottom of the coffin was filled with cement; the body was then replaced in the coffin and completely covered with the cement. It was Holmes's idea that this cement would harden around his body and prevent any attempt at grave robbery. The coffin was left in the receiving vault under the guard of two watchmen who will remain on duty all night. To-morrow afternoon the body will be interred in a grave in the cemetery, and it is probable that at that time religious services will be conducted by Father Dailey.

Holmes made no will and left no confession. This is according to Mr. Rotan. He says he knows Holmes made no will, and, while the murderer gave him this morning a big bundle of papers, the lawyer says he is confident that these papers relate only to private business matters. As yet Mr. Rotan has had no opportunity to examine them.

The two women referred to by Holmes in his confession from the scaffold were Julia Connor of Chicago, who, with her daughter, was believed to have been murdered by him, and Emily Cigrand of Anderson, Ind.

Bones of Holmes's Victims.

BY THE NEW YORK TIMES | SEPT. 18, 1896

CHICAGO, SEPT. 17. — A lot of bones, it is not yet known whether they represent one or two women, have been dug up not far from the house formerly occupied by the murderer, H. H. Holmes, at Evanston.

For six consecutive nights Mrs. Andrew Parker of 2044 Evanston Avenue dreamed of unconfined bodies, and she induced her husband to dig in the spot indicated by the dream, 150 yards from her house. He found nothing, but Mrs. Parker's dream came again last night, more real than ever. This morning her husband again dug, and found a skull, several ribs, and the arm and leg bones of a woman.

The Evanston police examined the bones and claim to have evidence that they are the remains of either one or both of the Williams sisters, supposed to be Holmes's victims.

CHAPTER 3

Son of Sam: David Berkowitz

Despite the largest manhunt in New York City history, the "Son of Sam" murders terrorized New Yorkers between July 1976 and August 1977. The killer targeted young couples and friends talking in parked cars, murdering six people and wounding seven more with a .44-caliber revolver. He left behind letters mocking police efforts, taunting them to find him. These letters were widely publicized, helping Son of Sam — David Berkowitz — gain notoriety around the world. Serving six consecutive life sentences, Berkowitz remains one of the most notorious serial killers in history.

Police Get a 2d Note Signed by 'Son of Sam' in .44-Caliber Killings

BY THE NEW YORK TIMES | JUNE 3, 1977

THE POLICE HAVE received a second letter signed "Son of Sam" from the man they believe to be the killer who used a 44-caliber pistol to slay five victims in Queens and the Bronx.

The handwritten letter, which warns that there will be more slayings because of a compulsion to kill, was mailed to Jimmy Breslin, the columnist for The Daily News, who yesterday turned it over to Deputy Inspector Timothy J. Dowd, who is in charge of the investigation.

The police said that they were "almost certain" that the second letter was from the same so-called "Son of Sam," but that it would take at least 72 hours for tests to be completed at police laboratories to be certain.

The letter was described as lengthy and containing emotional references to Donna Laurie, 18 years old, who was shot to death last July 29 while seated in a car with a girlfriend, Jody Valente, outside her home in the Baychester section of the Bronx. She was the first victim.

Beneath the "Son of Sam" signature was a hand-written symbol, an X-shaped mark with the biological signs for male and female. Above the X was a cross and the initial S.

The first letter from the so-called "Son of Sam" was found by the police at the scene of the slaying of Valentina Suriani, 18 years old, and Alesander Esau; 20, who were killed April 17, while seated in a car near the girl's home.

The police said yesterday they could report no new leads in the case. However, they said they were making progress.

'Son of Sam' Adds Four Names in New Letter, Police Disclose

BY THE NEW YORK TIMES | **JUNE 6, 1977**

THE POLICE HAVE released part of a second letter from "Son of Sam" in the hope that it may help them find the man who used a .44-caliber pistol to murder five people in the Bronx and Queens.

The writer of the letter included four nicknames in addition to "Son of Sam." They were "the Duke of Death," "the Wicked King Wicker," "the Twenty-Two Disciples of Hell" and "John 'Wheaties' — Rapist and Suffocater of Young Girls."

The letter warns that there will probably be more slayings because of a compulsion to kill. "I am still here," it says. "Like a spirit roaming the night … I will see you at the next job. Or, should I say you will see my handiwork at the next job?"

The police noted that all the words in the letter were correctly spelled, that it was properly punctuated and that it was printed in a highly stylized manner, as if by a draftsman or cartoonist. The police asked that anyone who might have any information on the letter or slayings to call them at 961-9613.

Cry for Help Wakes Up
a Brooklyn Neighborhood

BY ERIC PACE | AUG. 1, 1977

"HIS VOICE WAS sort of high, like a little boy's voice, and he was screaming, 'Help me! Don't let me die!' " a 32-year-old Brooklyn housewife recalled yesterday.

She was one of the neighborhood residents who had gently slipped towels under the body of 20-year-old Robert Violante as he lay bleeding on a sidewalk early yesterday morning. Another neighbor comforted Stacy Moscowitz, 20, as she slumped, wounded and dazed, in a car nearby.

The people of the Bath Beach section of Brooklyn were quick to rush out of their homes yesterday morning and give help when the .44-caliber killer ambushed the young couple parked beside a lamppost in a neighborhood trysting spot.

The humid air, stirred by breezes from Gravesend Bay, spread the sound of the horn on the couple's car when it suddenly began to blare.

Mr. Violante apparently leaned on the horn button, trying to attract attention, after the attacker had crept up to the brown Buick, pumped four shots into it and stolen off on foot through the shadows of nearby Dyker Beach Park.

"It was this weird, long honking sound," recalled Stephanie Nuccio, 15 years old, of 8867 Bay 16th Street, grimacing with horror.

Seconds later, when a neighborhood resident named Dotti rushed to her window, awakened by the noise, she saw nothing strange in the light of the street lamp, except that the Buick's brake lights were flickering on and off.

"Then I saw the guy get out of the car; he had on a blue shirt and blue pants, and there was this big dark stain on his clothes," she said later, hooking her hands tensely in her blue jeans. "He was screaming with the pain, saying, 'Help me!' "

Dotti and her 34-year-old husband, David, threw on clothes and raced to the Buick. Mr. Violante, on his feet, lurched back toward the car, smearing its top with his blood, and tottered into the lamp-post.

The neighborhood quickly came alive. Gently, one man got Mr. Violante to lie down and wait for medical help: he lay, face up, on the gritty sidewalk beside the stretch of lawn that adjoins the parkway's inland side.

"Now the wounded guy was screaming, 'Where is the ambulance, where is it?' "David said.

TOWELS BROUGHT OUT

Another neighbor brought out towels, Dotti recalled, and tried to staunch Miss Moscowitz's bleeding as the slim victim sagged against the seat, her head still more or less erect.

Mr. Violante seemed to be having trouble breathing, and a police-man helped to turn his body over, face down.

"You try to do what you can to help," said Dotti, a wiry woman with glasses and a strong face. "So I put a towel under his face so it wouldn't get in the dirt and weeds. His face was all swollen by then."

Meanwhile, bystanders helped Miss Moscowitz to get out of the car and coaxed her to lie down on a stretcher, though she wanted to walk around, Dotti recalled. Within 15 or 20 minutes the couple had been carried off by ambulance to Coney Island Hospital. They were then transferred to Kings County Hospital.

For Dotti and her husband and for other residents of the quiet, tree-shaded reaches of south west Brooklyn, neighborliness soon gave way to pangs of fear and horror. Then came criticism of the police, talk of forming vigilante squads, calls for vengeance.

Dozens of policemen, perspiration pouring from their faces, were searching for bullets and other clues around the shooting site, near Shore Parkway and Bay 14th Street, but anxiety was running so high by midday yesterday that Dotti and David insisted on withholding their last name. Other worried neighbors did the same, for fear the attacker might come back and do them harm.

By early morning the neighborhood, which is home to mostly Italian-American and Jewish families, was in tension's grip. Youths stared grimly at where the police from the Emergency Squad raked through the lawns beside the parkway, looking for the missing fourth bullet. One bullet was found in the car's steering column, detectives said, and the two others in the victim's bodies.

Further north, shady East Fifth Street, neighbors looked silently up at the trim brick facade of the two-family building, 1740 East Fifth, where Miss Moskowitz lived with her family.

A face peered out through the green plastic curtaining behind the balcony, then Miss Moskowitz's 16-year-old sister, Ricki, stepped out — her great dark eyes were impassive — flanked by a policeman.

"I really can't talk, I can't answer any questions," she said and disappeared, as a second policeman looked out a small window in the front door.

"Son of Sam — I thought he might make trouble in Brooklyn some-time, but never in this street, this is our home," said Vincent Simonelli of 1710 East Fifth Street. A burly telephone company worker, he was one of the neighbors keeping a kind of vigil under the leafy trees.

Another neighbor, Mark Rubin, an art director, who lives at 1707 East Fifth Street, said, "It's scary, this maniac striking, it's like he's saying he can strike anywhere. I tell my wife to be careful, but there's no way of really protecting yourself."

Who Is Really Behind That .44? Police Pursuing Many Theories

BY HOWARD BLUM | AUG. 3, 1977

WHO IS THE "Son of Sam"?

Detectives are actively pursuing theories that the .44-caliber killer could be a laid-off policeman, a freelance journalist, a taxi driver or a compulsive walker who roams the city day and night.

Seventy-five detectives assigned to the special homicide task force in the 109th Precinct in Queens have worked in around-the-clock shifts to identify the psychopath who has killed six victims and wounded seven others.

It is a search in which detectives have knocked on hundreds of doors throughout New York City, answered thousands of phone calls from around the world, studied countless photographs of young men in high school and college yearbooks and listened patiently to astrologers, seers, hypnotists and numerologists. It is also a search in which a detective sustained a black eye for attempting to interview one suspect. Another detective complains that he even dreams about the Son of Sam at night, and a third spent a weekend tailing a Staten Island man he was certain the killer.

And it is a search that has produced more than 3,000 suspects — none of whom the police, after months of work, now believe is Son of Sam.

'A FEW THINGS WE KNOW'

"We have a few things we know for sure," said Inspector Timothy Dowd, head of the task force. "We have a few theories. But we have no solid leads. It's all very frustrating."

The police have built their investigation on these "few things we

Different composite sketches of the suspect.

know for sure." However, even these things become less certain or raise other questions under the task force's intense scrutiny. Among the facts in the .44-caliber case are the following:

• The eight dates when the killer has struck — Any suspect is eliminated if he can produce an alibi for any of these dates. However, the task force is not certain these are the only times the killer has shot at potential victims. Detective Gerald Shevlin of the task force said: "Suppose he shot a couple of times and the bullet missed and the people didn't want to report it, or thought the shots were a car backfiring. That's a very real possibility which knocks the hell out of a lot of our theories."

• The gun — "The .44-caliber Bulldog revolver is our most tangible clue," Inspector Dowd said. However, this "tangible" clue has produced intangible results. The police have attempted to trace the entire 28,000 total of .44-caliber Charter Arms Bulldog Revolvers ever produced — including the 600 guns reported stolen — without establishing any key suspects.

• Stockpile of ammunition — Detective Frank Pergola said: "We also know this guy must have a stockpile of ammunition. He's fired 32 times so far without going into stores to buy more ammo."

• The description of the killer — Interviews with survivors and eye-witnesses, including some conducted under hypnosis, have resulted in four different drawings by police artists of the killer. In these composite sketches, the suspect is a white male between 20 and 35 years old, whose height ranges from 5 feet 7 inches to 6 feet 2 inches and who weighs anywhere from 150 to 220 pounds. The descriptions are so varied that the police are now considering the possibility that the killer wears various disguises, including wigs and mustaches and has gained weight to complicate further his identification.

• The two letters the killer has written — These letters, one of which was left at the scene of a shooting and the other of which was sent to Jimmy Breslin, a columnist for The Daily News, have provided the police with psychological insights into the killer's identity. In addition, the police are taking handwriting samples from each suspect to compare with the highly stylized lettering in the two messages. The police have used those four areas of what is known to attempt to establish the identity of the killer. Among the theories the task force is actively pursuing are the following:

The killer could be a laid-off policeman. This theory is favored because the victim has a knowledge of guns, fires with accuracy from a combat stance, has knowledge of neighborhoods and in one letter referred to the National Crime Information Center, a computer bank of criminal records maintained by the Federal Bureau of Investigation. Critics of this theory say that any veteran has a knowledge of guns and that the killer might not be firing from a combat stance but simply crouching to fire into the window of a parked car.

The killer could be a freelance journalist. In his letters Son of Sam writes with clarity and follows punctuation rules, including the use of a semicolon. The possibility that the killer is a freelancer would also help explain why he has not been identified by his fellow workers who might have noticed similarities between the killer and the composite sketches. The police also believe that as a journalist the killer could freely return to the scene of the crimes.

The killer is a taxi driver. This theory would explain his knowledge of neighborhoods and escape routes in the city. It would also provide the killer with a get-away vehicle that might not be noticed and with an occupation that would provide both the anonymity and the flexible schedule required to plan the eight attacks.

The killer is a compulsive walker. The police have never established that the killer leaves the scene of each shooting by car. Detective units, after consultations with psychiatrists, are therefore working on the assumption that the murderer is a psychopath who walks about the city, a common manifestation of severe psychosis. The fact that the killer is a walker would also explain his knowledge of neighborhoods and escape routes. And a man who is a compulsive walker might describe himself — as the killer did in one letter — as "a spirit roaming the night." Last week the police were actively investigating a man who walked from Forest Hills to New Jersey in an afternoon.

Suspect in 'Son of Sam' Murders Arrested in Yonkers

BY ROBERT D. MCFADDEN | AUG. 11, 1977

A 24-YEAR-OLD POSTAL EMPLOYEE said by the police to be the "Son of Sam," the .44-caliber killer who took the lives of six young people and wounded seven others in a year-long reign of terror in New York City, was taken into custody late last night in Yonkers, just north of the city.

The suspect was identified as David Berkowitz of 35 Pine Street in Yonkers. He was said to have been traced through a car allegedly used in the getaways from eight attacks in the Bronx, Queens and, most recently, in Brooklyn.

When seized, according to the police, Mr. Berkowitz was advised of his rights by arresting officers and responded: "Well, you've got me."

The .44-caliber Charter Arms Bulldog revolver, which ballistics experts said had been used in all of the attacks, was recovered, the police said.

The suspect was rushed from Yonkers to New York City Police Headquarters after his arrest and authorities said he would be booked for the ambush murder of Stacy Moskowitz, 21, and the blinding of her date, Robert Violante, 20, in his latest alleged attack on July 31.

The police said early today that, although the suspect had made some admissions, the motive for the crimes remained unclear. The suspect was described by the police as a loner whose father, Nat, is retired and living in Miami and whose mother is deceased.

The police said the suspect was a graduate of Columbus High School in the Bronx, had attended the Bronx Community College for one year and had served with the Army in Korea.

Mayor Beame, during a 1:40 A.M. news conference in Police Headquarters in Lower Manhattan declared:

"I am very pleased to announce that the people of the City of New

Suspect in slayings, identified by police as David Berkowitz, being escorted into Police Headquarters this morning.

York can rest easy tonight because police have captured a man they believe to be the Son of Sam."

First Deputy Police Commissioner James Taylor earlier had said: "We have him."

Chief of Detectives John L. Keenan, at the headquarters news conference, said the suspect had been traced after detectives had looked into every summons given to cars parked in the vicinity of the last shooting, at Bay 14th Street and Shore Parkway in the Bath Beach section of Brooklyn.

GUN FOUND IN CAR

One ticket, for illegal parking at a fire hydrant, was given to a cream-colored Ford Galaxy sedan. The police traced the car, and yesterday found it parked in front of 35 Pine Street in Yonkers.

Detectives who found the car said they had looked inside and had seen the butt of a machine gun sticking out of a gunny sack. They said they had also found a letter with printing that resembled that on the two letters known to have been written by the killer, as well as a message later found in the suspect's apartment.

The written message contained the following passage:

"Because Craig is Craig, so must the streets be filled with crime (death) and huge drops of lead poured down upon her head until she was dead — Yet the cats still come out at night to mate and the sparrows still sing in the morning."

Jubilation greeted word of the suspect's apprehension at Police Headquarters and at the 109th Precinct in Queens, the headquarters of a 300-member task force that had mounted one of the largest — and most frustrating — manhunts in the city's history.

The reference to "Craig" was unclear. However, Craig Glassman, a Westchester County deputy sheriff was one of the 15 policemen from Yonkers, New York City and Westchester who aided in the suspect's arrest.

Mr. Glassman said last night that, as a former resident of the building where Mr. Berkowitz lives, he had been watching the man for some time, not as a "Son of Sam" suspect, but because he had received a number of threatening letters and believed Mr. Berkowitz had been sending them.

GLASSMAN PASSES ON NAME

However, the publication of the Police Department's latest and most detailed sketch of the suspect prompted Mr. Glassman to pass on Mr. Berkowitz's name to the city police. The police, in turn, had a record of a parking ticket issued to Mr. Berkowitz's car in the area of and at the time of the last shooting.

Armed with a search warrant, policemen from Yonkers, Westchester County and New York City surrounded the six-story apartment building at 35 Pine Street sometime after 10 P.M. But before they could enter, Mr. Berkowitz emerged from his apartment and was apprehended without a struggle.

Taken by unmarked car in a short motorcade of police vehicles to headquarters at 1 Police Plaza near City Hall in lower Manhattan, Mr. Berkowitz, his hands manacled behind him, smiled wanly as he was hustled by detectives through a crowd of into a side entrance.

He was clad in a light blue shirt with white stripes, and wore blue jeans. He was about 5 feet 7 or 8 inches tall and appeared to be huskily built.

The suspect had dark curly hair and appeared to resemble the composite sketch the police had issued on Tuesday, along with a more precise description. The police said they had received more than 1,800 calls supplying tips and clues as a result of the new sketch and description.

Detectives who had worked on the case disclosed last night that a fingerprint and a palm print believed to be those of the killer had been in the possession of investigators for some time.

At least one fingerprint had been obtained from a letter sent last spring to Jimmy Breslin, the columnist for The Daily News, and a palm print had been obtained from a car in one of the killer's ambush shootings.

There was no word early this morning on whether these prints had been compared with those of the suspect seized last night.

However, various police officials, who are customarily circumspect in their characterizations of suspects, last night spoke with seeming confidence that the mysterious and elusive Son of Sam had at last been captured.

"There's no doubt," said Capt. Joseph Borelli, a member of the task force that has hunted the killer. "It's him."

In addition to the .44 caliber bulldog revolver found in Mr. Berkowitz's car, the police said a .45 caliber submachine gun was found in the car and another submachine gun in the apartment. The revolver was said to be loaded and lying next to the driver's seat.

The killer's random attacks have terrorized New Yorkers for more than a year, prompting women to change hairstyles and young people to avoid secluded trysting sites that had been the scenes of the shootings.

The Suspect Is Quoted on Killings: 'It Was a Command . . . I Had a Sign'

BY HOWARD BLUM | AUG. 12, 1977

"FOR MORE THAN a year I had been hoping for just one thing — a chance to talk to the 'Son of Sam,' a chance to ask him why," said Detective Gerald Shevlin. He was part of the special homicide task force that had conducted the search for the .44-caliber killer, the largest manhunt in New York's history.

At a little after 2 o'clock yesterday morning, Detective Shevlin had his chance.

Ten detectives, officers who had been assigned to the task force headed by Inspector Timothy Dowd since its formation after the .44-caliber killer claimed his fourth and fifth murder victims in April, crowded into Room 1312 in Police Headquarters and for one-half hour "fired every question we could think of" at the 24-year-old suspect, David Berkowitz of Yonkers.

"From the beginning I had just wanted 10 minutes with him in a motel room so I could find out about the guy I had been hunting for six months," Detective Shevlin said. "Room 1312 became our motel room. We went in there and wrapped up all the loose ends."

"Berkowitz was very cooperative," said Sgt. Joseph Coffey who, along with Sgt. Richard Conlon, was directing the questioning. "He was talkative and calm and answered whatever we asked."

'IT WAS A COMMAND'

But, as task-force members formed a semicircle around the suspect seated in the chief of detectives's office, an orderly interrogation was abandoned as detectives eagerly tried to find the answers to questions they had been pondering for more than a year.

"Why? Why did you kill them?" a detective asked the suspect.

"It was a command," a detective reported Mr. Berkowitz as

responding. "I had a sign and I followed it. Sam told me what to do and I did it."

Sam, the 24-year-old postal worker explained in a passive voice, is Sam Carr, a neighbor in Yonkers, "who really is a man who lived 6,000 years ago."

"I got the messages through his dog," Mr. Berkowitz said. "He told me to kill. Sam is the devil." Mr. Carr is a neighbor whose dog Mr. Berkowitz is accused of having shot.

At this point in the interrogation, some of the detectives expressed doubt that they were questioning the right man.

"But," said a detective, "when we asked him about the letter he left after the murder of Valentina Suriani [last April 17], he knew things that only Sam could have known."

The suspect was asked how the letter was signed.

"The Monster," he responded.

"What did you call yourself in the note?"

"The Chubby Behemoth."

"Did you say anything about Queens?"

"I wrote that Queens girls are prettier."

Hours later, Inspector Dowd, the commander of the task force, explained the questioning on the letter as detectives gathered around a desk turned into a bar in the chief of detectives's office:

"It's because we always knew tonight would come that I never released the first letter to the press," he said.

Earlier, the detectives had Mr. Berkowitz reconstruct each of the 44-caliber killer's eight attacks.

The suspect, according to officers at the interrogation, said he was "out driving every night since last July [1976] looking for a sign to kill."

"The situation would be perfect," the suspect was quoted as having said. "I would find a parking place for my car right away. It was things like that which convinced me it was commanded."

"Then when I got a calling," he said, "I went looking for a spot."

Mr. Berkowitz, who, said a "buddy In Houston" had bought the gun for him, reportedly told the police he had the Charter Arms Bulldog revolver, the 44-caliber weapon the police say was used as the murder weapon, "for about a month" before the first shooting.

As the suspect detailed the attacks, the police learned that many of the theories — and even a few aspects of the investigation that they had accepted as facts — were unsubstantiated. For example, according to detectives, Mr. Berkowitz made the following statements:

• He fired one-handed for the first three attacks, not in the two-hand combat-style position, as the police believed.

• On at least two occasions, he fired five times, emptying the 44-caliber revolver. He did not keep one bullet in the chamber, as the police believed.

• He never went inside a discotheque.

• He never wore a wig.

• The attacks were totally random, his targets always the young girls.

• He insisted he was never jilted by a girlfriend. His only explanation for the attacks was that "they were commanded."

NEVER SHOT THROUGH BAG

Speaking in terse sentences, the suspect explained how he always parked about a block and a half away from the scene of each attack "and then ran like hell to my car."

He said he had kept his revolver in a plastic bag, but never shot through as police had theorized.

Why did he carry his gun in a plastic bag?

"I don't believe in holsters," the police quoted Mr. Berkowitz as stating, his face breaking out in a smirk.

The constant hurling of questions at the suspect was interrupted, however, as Mr. Berkowitz explained what he had planned to do on the night when he was captured.

"I was going out to kill in the Bronx," he allegedly explained. "I was going to look in Riverdale."

And then Mr. Berkowitz for the first time posed a question: "Do you know why I had a machine gun with me tonight?"

"I'll tell you," he said: "I wanted to get into a shootout. I wanted to get killed, but I wanted to take some cops with me."

When the suspect was asked why letters were found in his car addressed to the Suffolk County police, he said he had spent last weekend driving through Westhampton, L.I., searching for a victim. "But," he was quoted by the police, "I didn't get a sign."

Mr. Berkowitz also told the police how he had visited the sites where he had murdered Donna Lauria, in the Bronx on July 29, 1976, and Christine Freund last Jan. 30 in Forest Hills, Queens, a couple of times after the shootings.

SOUGHT VICTIM'S GRAVE

He also went, the detectives related, to St. Raymond's Cemetery to visit the grave of Miss Laurie, his first victim.

"But," he explained, "the grave was impossible to find."

Why did he want to go to the grave?

"I felt like it," Mr. Berkowitz allegedly responded.

"He also told us that the length of hair, the color — all that had nothing to do with his picking out victims," said a detective.

In fact, Stacy Moskowitz, the last victim, was not even his target that night, the police reported.

"He had planned to get the girl 'Tommy Z.' was sitting with," the detective continued, referring to the young man who had witnessed the murder of Miss Moskowitz through his rear-view mirror. "But when Tommy Z. moved his car into a darker spot, Berkowitz told us he changed his target."

Another detective added that Robert Violante, the young man who was seriously wounded when Miss Moskowitz was shot on July 31 in the Bath Beach section of Brooklyn, had told the police about a man

On the seat of David Berkowitz's car are maps, a bottle, an automobile distributor cap and a copy of the parking ticket that led to his arrest.

who had been sitting on the swings for nearly an hour in the park near where the couple's car was parked.

"It was while we were questioning Berkowitz that we realized he was the guy on the swings," the detective explained. "Robert Violante had been staring at the guy who was going to shoot him all night, except he didn't know it."

The suspect also answered questions about specific attacks.

Why, he was asked, had he murdered Virginia Voskerichian as she walked home alone from the subway on a Tuesday night? She did not fit into the 44-caliber killer's pattern.

"It was commanded," the suspect allegedly replied.

When asked if he had any remorse he reportedly said, "No, why should I?"

Suspect Is Emerging as a Study in Extreme and Varied Contrast

BY ROBERT D. MCFADDEN | AUG. 13, 1977

THE WORLD OF David Richard Berkowitz has been Jewish and Christian, militaristic and dovish, full of rigidities yet strangely formless, outwardly friendly but cryptically hostile. It has been touched by drugs and loneliness, love and tragedy.

Some people have known him to be thoughtful and gentle, though shy and seemingly troubled. But according to the police, he is the "Son of Sam," whose reign of terror in New York City claimed the lives of six young people and left others paralyzed, blind and otherwise scarred for life.

As the details of the enigmatic life of the 24-year-old postal clerk emerged, there appeared to have been no single incident or trauma that might explain his abrupt transformation little more than a year ago from the quiet suburbanite that he was to the murderous night stalker that the police say that he became.

From friends, former Army buddies, neighbors, former teachers and others who have known him, the descriptions seem to suit no theme — he was "sullen," "friendly," "average," "extreme," "sweet," "a loner," "a team player" — all pieces that seem to come from many jigsaw puzzles, not one.

During the hunt for the .44-caliber killer, the police issued a probable profile that suggested there were "religious aspects" in his thinking and hints of "demonic possession and compulsion," and that characterized him as shy, odd, troubled in relationships with young women, probably Christian and fairly well-educated.

In retrospect, the assessment came close. Religious cross-currents have played a major role in shaping the suspect's personality; there are references to Satan and demons in anonymous notes allegedly written by him, and, in recent years, he has been a loner. He graduated from

Christopher Columbus High School in the Bronx and attended Bronx Community College for a semester. But these elements only begin to touch on the complexities.

The contradictions in his life began virtually in his infancy. He was born in Brooklyn on June 1, 1953, the son of Tony and Betty Falco, but he was given up for adoption at the age of 17 months to Nathan and Pearl Berkowitz, a childless couple from the Bronx, who changed his name from Richard David Falco to David Richard Berkowitz.

He was raised in a Jewish household and was bar mitzvahed at the age of 13 years at Temple Adath Israel on the Grand Concourse in the Bronx. He attended Public School 77, where he was known as a prankster.

The elder Mr. Berkowitz ran a hardware store, and, although the family lived modestly in a small apartment, the adoptive parents were said by acquaintances to have been loving toward and sensitive about the needs of young David. Some said David Berkowitz was severely affected by the death of Mrs. Berkowitz on Oct. 5, 1967. He was 14 at the time.

'HE LIKED UNIFORMS'

His high school years were undistinguished scholastically, though he was said to have enjoyed and excelled in gymnasium classes and in baseball. In 1969, while he was still in high school, he and his father moved to Co-op City, the sprawling development in the northeastern Bronx. There, they lived in a four-and-a-half-room apartment on the 17th floor of 170 Dreiser Loop.

Bruce Handler, who lived on the floor below, recalled that he and David and two other youths organized a volunteer fire company in Co-op City in 1970, when the Fire Department had had no on-site facility. The youths put out brush fires and turned in alarms, occasionally helping at the scene of apartment fires before regular firemen arrived.

"He was dedicated," Mr. Handler said. "Once in 1970, he ran up 16 flights because he thought someone was still up there during a fire … He liked uniforms."

During this time, Mr. Berkowitz often expressed an ambition that he could someday be a fireman, Mr. Handler said.

In October 1970, in a similar vein, Mr. Berkowitz joined an auxiliary police unit as a trainee, and he accompanied members on unarmed patrols in his neighborhood.

His father wanted him to go to college after his high school graduation in June 1971, but Mr. Berkowitz instead enlisted in the Army for three years — a step that was to bring dramatic changes in his outlook and his personality.

He enlisted on June 23, 1971, took basic training at Fort Dix, N. J., advanced infantry training at Fort Polk, La., and then served a year in South Korea. His final 18 months of a three-year hitch was spent at Fort Knox, Ky.

Gary Corrigan, an engineer with WNEW-TV, had been with Mr. Berkowitz at Fort Dix and recalled that Mr. Berkowitz went absent without leave on the first weekend of basic training, but later came back dejected.

"I had the impression that he had had some type of disappointment with his girlfriend or something," Mr. Corrigan said. After that incident, Mr. Berkowitz took no more leave, and, when others did, "Berk just stayed in the barracks and spit-shined his combat boots," Mr. Corrigan said.

Mr. Corrigan said that, inexplicably, Mr. Berkowitz "didn't seem to be the gung-ho type" and "by and large, he was a dove," but at one point signed up for tough airborne training [he failed to get the assignment] and liked to garnish his uniform with optional insignia purchased from the post exchange. He was what soldiers call a "P. X. hero," Mr. Corrigan said.

Mr. Berkowitz received firearms training, but achieved no high rating for marksmanship and no training in sidearms, according to Army records.

From Korea, where he had been sent as a Specialist 4, Mr. Berkowitz sent letters home to friends that suggested his conservative views were turning liberal. There are no Army records indicating that he had used drugs in Korea, but two friends — one an Army buddy and the second a friend from the Bronx — said later that he had bragged about using stimulant and depressant pills and, on occasion, LSD, a hallucinogen.

During his Korean service, he was reduced in rank to private first class after he missed a convoy, but he later regained his specialist rating.

At Fort Knox, where Mr. Berkowitz was stationed upon returning from Korea, a buddy, Paul Billow, now a 25-year-old security guard in Saginaw, Mich., said Mr. Berkowitz had bragged about using pills, but not LSD, in Korea. He added that Mr. Berkowitz "seemed like he had been completely recovered from all that when I met him, though."

Mr. Billow said Mr. Berkowitz seemed to change drastically in other ways — from gregarious to reclusive, and toward a revivalist form of the Baptist religion. He was baptized, went to revival meetings and, according to Mr. Billow, "tried to convert others."

COMPLAINED ABOUT DOG

"He told me that if I did not take Jesus Christ as my personal savior, I'd be damned," Mr. Billow recalled. But two months before leaving Fort Knox, Mr. Berkowitz underwent still another personality change, Mr. Billow said. "He started to swear," he suggested. "Maybe he went back to drugs … because somebody doesn't change like that overnight."

Mr. Berkowitz, after being discharged, returned to New York City, took a job as an unarmed guard with I.B.I. Security Services Agency, and moved back for a while with his father at Co-op City. "The Army changed him," said his old Co-op City friend, Mr. Handler. "When he came back he was completely introverted … he looked glassy-eyed, as if he was in a world of his own."

In 1975, when his father retired and moved to Florida, David Berkowitz moved into a studio apartment at 2161 Barnes Avenue in the Bronx for about six months. During that time, he apparently grew more introspective. Neighbors barely remembered him, but a friend said: "He used to laugh a lot by himself…. He'd roar and couldn't stop, but he wouldn't tell you anything about it."

In February 1976, he took an apartment in a home at 171 Coligni Avenue in New Rochelle, N.Y., but moved out a few months later after complaining bitterly about the barking of his landlady's dog. She later got a vaguely threatening letter, apparently, she believes, from Mr. Berkowitz.

About 16 months ago, Mr. Berkowitz rented the $230-a-month studio at 35 Pine Street in Yonkers, where he was arrested Wednesday night. His life there is largely a mystery, separated into what authorities now say were divergently inward and outward aspects.

He became a postal clerk last March, and co-workers say he appeared regularly and seemed genial, if quiet. But behind his locked apartment door, in the streets at night and in his mind, the authorities say, another personality was operating.

Letter from Berkowitz
Says He Killed 6 Persons

BY THE NEW YORK TIMES | SEPT. 20, 1977

IN A LETTER written from his hospital cell, David R. Berkowitz, the man accused of being the 44-caliber killer, says he killed six young people over the last year.

"When I killed I really saved many lives," the 24-year-old Mr. Berkowitz wrote in a letter sent to The New York Post. "You will understand later."

In the letter, he asks the world to understand the "forces of darkness and evil." He refers to Sam Carr, the "Sam" of Mr. Berkowitz's "Son of Sam" obsession, and Craig Glassman, both former Yonkers neighbors, as "demons."

Mr. Berkowitz's lawyers, Leon Stern and Ira Jultak, said they were shocked to learn their client had sent a letter to The Post and would try to stop any further messages. Mr. Stern said that "any one who writes letters like that when he has these indictments pending is obviously not competent to stand trial."

Chief of Detectives John Keenan said he had no doubt the letter was from Mr. Berkowitz.

Judgment on Son of Sam

EDITORIAL | BY THE NEW YORK TIMES | MAY 11, 1978

FOR ALL ITS SHORTCOMINGS, the courtroom ceremony in which David Berkowitz pleaded guilty to six murders has produced a reasonable result. The defendant, for reasons sufficient to himself, waived all defenses including the obvious one of insanity and admitted responsibility for the homicides that so frightened New Yorkers and appalled the world. He was judged competent to enter the pleas after persuading the court he understood his situation and was able to take part in his own defense.

Some grounds for uneasiness remain. The theatrical entrances and exits of judges from Brooklyn, the Bronx and Queens, each to receive the guilty pleas for crimes committed in his jurisdiction, were bizarre. The ritual questions and answers to leave a public record on matters of competence and guilt carefully avoided any reference to "Son of Sam" or the "demons" that Mr. Berkowitz had said were plaguing him and thus failed to explore all aspects of the case. Those who want this wretched defendant executed will find support for capital punishment in this case. Those who believe that only an insane person could have committed such atrocities will deplore a verdict of guilty even though the accused demands it.

Yet it was better to bring the judges to Mr. Berkowitz than to parade him through the boroughs he once terrorized, and the court had already determined that whatever "demons" possessed him at the time of his crimes were not now interfering with his capacity to defend himself.

Public safety and humanity now require that David Berkowitz be securely confined and provided with appropriate psychiatric care. No ending to this case could have satisfied everyone, but the courts seem to have achieved the least unsatisfactory solution.

CHAPTER 4

John Wayne Gacy

John Wayne Gacy, a well-liked contractor in Cook County,
Ill., shocked his family, his community and the world when
police dug up the decayed bodies of 29 teenage boys
and young men that he had sexually abused, tortured and
killed between 1972 and 1978. Convicted of a total of 33
murders, Gacy began painting while on Death Row. He was
executed in 1994. His paintings are still in circulation.

4 More Bodies Found Under House of Contractor, Bringing Total to 9

BY DOUGLAS E. KNEELAND | DEC. 27, 1978

KNOLLWOOD PARK TOWNSHIP, ILL., DEC. 26 — A light dusting of new Christmas snow sparkled under a bright December sun in this quiet suburb of Chicago today as Cook County Sheriffs investigators unearthed four more skeletons from the crawl space under the home of a pudgy contractor who reveled in playing a clown at children's parties.

The discoveries today brought to nine the number of bodies found since Friday under the garage section of the neat, three-bedroom, brick-fronted home of John Wayne Gacy.

Mr. Gacy, 36 years old, twice married and twice divorced, once served 18 months in an Iowa prison for sodomy with a teen-aged boy. He is being held without bail now on charges that he murdered a Des Plaines, Ill., youth earlier this month.

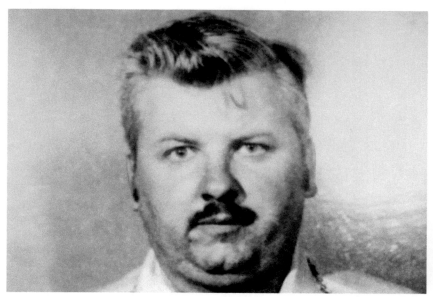

Police photo of John Wayne Gacy, 37. Gacy is being held for questioning in connection with the discovery of five badly decomposed bodies found in the crawl space of his home.

The body of the youth, Robert Piest, 15, still has not been recovered. But investigators say that Mr. Gacy confessed, in a rambling statement after the discovery of the first three skeletons Friday, to strangling the youth and throwing his body into the Des Plaines River.

FROM 25 TO 32 BODIES POSSIBLE

He also is said to have told investigators that he had killed as many as 32 young men over the last four years after having sexual relations with them. He was quoted as saying that he tossed the bodies of at least five others into the river but that most were buried under his house.

"Apparently he was telling the truth," said Sgt. Howard Anderson of the Sheriff's Department, who reported the latest discoveries. "He's changed his numbers somewhat — there could be 32, but there might be only 25. We expect to uncover three or four a day and we expect to be there for more than a few days."

Investigators carry the remains of a body found beneath the garage floor of the home of John Wayne Gacy in December 1978.

"I think, when this whole thing is over, you may be witnessing one of the most horrible crimes of the century," said Dr. Robert J. Stein, Cook County Medical Examiner, who was working with investigators in their painstaking search for more shallow graves in the crawl space, which measures about 30 by 40 feet.

Sergeant Anderson said a thorough check of young men who had been reported missing in the Chicago area indicated "there are seven, eight or nine people from this area who could be under the house."

SIGHT IDENTIFICATION IMPOSSIBLE

He said that no positive identification had been made of any of the bodies, whose decomposition had been hastened by spreading lime over them. "What we're uncovering is mostly skeletons," be explained. "It's impossible to make a sight identification.

"Just generally," he added, "the impression we get is that most of these would be from 1974 on up. But that could change; of course."

The Piest youth was employed part-time at a pharmacy at which Mr. Gacy had recently done some contracting work. Two of three other missing area youths that investigators consider possible victims once worked for Mr. Gacy.

The three, all from the Northwest Side of Chicago, were identified as John Butkovich, 18, Gregory Godzik, 17, and John A Szyk, 19.

Mr. Butkovich disappeared on the night of July 31, 1975, according to his parents, reportedly after having had an argument with Mr. Gacy over two weeks' pay the youth said he was owed.

Marko Butkovich, his father, said he repeatedly urged the police to investigate Mr. Gacy in connection with his son's disappearance but they kept assuring him that his son was alive because no body had been found.

"They tell me all that junk," he said angrily. "After a while they wouldn't return my calls. How many lives could have been saved?"

GODZIK MISSING SINCE LATE 1976

The Godzik youth disappeared on Dec. 11, 1976, two years to the day before Robert Piest disappeared after telling his mother he had to talk to a contractor about a summer job.

Mrs. John Godzik said of her son: "The last night he was home, he went out on a date. Gregory never came home." She also said that her son had always "liked this man Gacy," for whom he worked.

Wallets containing papers that identify the Szyk and Godzik youths have been found in Mr. Gacy's home, investigators say, but they do not know what link Mr. Szyk may have had with the suspect. He was reported missing on Jan. 26, 1977.

Sergeant Anderson said the Sheriff's Department was not yet ready to release the names of other area youths who were considered possible victims in the case. "As far as we're concerned, everybody's unidentified so far," he said.

BATTERY CASE STILL PENDING

From the beginning, investigators have assumed that some of the victims might be transients picked up as sexual partners, willing or unwilling.

Investigators believe most of the victims were unwilling sex partners. In a case that is still pending in local courts, a young Chicago youth filed a battery charge against Mr. Gacy, saying Mr. Gacy chloroformed, abducted and raped him last March.

The Sheriff's Department has been swamped by calls from hundreds of worried parents in this country and abroad. Sergeant Anderson suggested that they write instead, providing dental records and as thorough a description of their missing sons as possible. "Calling won't solve anything," he explained.

Over the long holiday weekend, weary sheriff's investigators had called a halt to the long hours of dismantling and digging that began with a search warrant's being issued in the Piest case and the subsequent discovery of bones in the crawl space under the house.

While the street was blockaded and the house sealed off, sightseers paraded by, even on Christmas Day, staring at the guarded building with its incongruous colored lights strung across the driveway.

SUSPECT IN COOK COUNTY HOSPITAL

The traffic dropped off some today, but about 50 bystanders joined journalists in the 19-degree chill to watch about two dozen sheriff's investigators and technicians enter and leave the house as the grim work of tearing up the flooring in search of bodies continued.

Meanwhile, Mr. Gacy continued to be held in an isolation room in the psychiatric ward of Cermak Memorial Hospital in the Cook County Jail complex. Robert Dean, director of the hospital, said that the suspect "hasn't been noisy or given hospital authorities any trouble, but does seem very depressed."

Here in this suburban residential area, stunned neighbors of Mr. Gacy, whose home was adorned with clown pictures and who enjoyed playing that role himself at children's gatherings, described the rotund, five-foot, seven-inch contractor as a "good, friendly and, generous man" who often entertained as many as 400 people at backyard parties.

Edward G. Grexa, a 53-year-old marble installer who lives next door, said he had "never suspected" his neighbor of wrongdoing. He added that on one occasion Mr. Gacy came in "at 2:30 A.M. with a bunch of lads and they were making so much noise that I had to ask them to quiet down."

SUSPECT GREW UP IN CHICAGO

Both Mr. Grexa and his wife, Lillie, said that Mr. Gacy frequently had teenage boys at his house and that they had always presumed that the youngsters were employed in his contracting work. Mr. Gacy, who grew up on the North Side of Chicago and attended a business college in the city after graduation from high school, was a shoe salesman in Springfield in the early 1960's.

After marrying, he moved to Waterloo, Iowa, where he managed fast-food franchises for his father-in-law and was active in the Jay-cees before his conviction on the sodomy charge and his subsequent divorce. He had two children by his first wife, who has remarried and has pleaded for anonymity.

On June 1, 1972, Mr. Gacy, who had returned to the Chicago area, married his second wife, the divorced mother of two daughters. Mr. Gacy and his second wife were divorced on March 2, 1976.

Bodies Found at Illinois Suspect's House Total 21

BY THE NEW YORK TIMES | DEC. 29, 1978

CHICAGO, DEC. 28 — Officers of the Cook County Sheriff's Department found six more bodies today under the suburban ranch-style home of John Wayne Gacy, who, investigators fear, may have killed as many as 32 young men over the last four years after having sexual relations with them.

This brought to 21 the number found on the grounds of Mr. Gacy's house.

Meanwhile, the suspect was being kept bound to his hospital bed to prevent him from "hurting anybody or hurting himself." However, Philip Hardiman of the Cook County Corrections Department denied a report that Mr. Gacy had attempted suicide.

Detectives in Des Plaines reported yesterday that they expected the death of a 19-year-old Chicago youth, Frank Landingin, whose body was found in the Des Plaines River on Dec. 12, to be linked to Mr. Gacy.

DIGGING TO CONTINUE

Technicians said today that they had dug out half of the area in a crawl space under the Gacy home and would continue to dig for several more days into what they believed to be more shallow graves.

Mr. Gacy, a 36-year-old building contractor who served an 18-month prison sentence in Iowa after a 1968 conviction for sodomy, is being held without bond and under tight security in the hospital wing of the Cook County jail.

Some residents near Mr. Gacy's home said that they had noticed many young men coming and going but had assumed that they were employed in his contracting business.

Mr. Gacy has been charged with the death of Robert Piest, 15, of Des Plaines and is scheduled to appear at a preliminary court hearing in Des Plaines tomorrow. The body has not been found, but Mr. Gacy has reportedly told investigators that he murdered the youth and threw his body into the Des Plaines River.

The Illinois State's Attorney's Office, meanwhile, said today that it had begun to compile a long list of possible witnesses to Mr. Gacy's behavior and associations over the last four years. Terry Sullivan, an Assistant State's Attorney who has been assigned to the case, said, "We are not anticipating anything at this time" but added that a plea of not guilty because of insanity was not unexpected.

Parents of Missing Youths Hope, Fear — and Wait

BY DOUGLAS E. KNEELAND | DEC. 31, 1978

CHICAGO, DEC. 30 — The waiting and the wondering are a painful blend of hope and fear for thousands of parents all across the country.

As Cook County Sheriff's investigators press on, almost methodically now, with the search that since Dec. 22 has yielded 27 bodies at the home of John Wayne Gacy, the daily reports at the medical examiner's office have been monotonously the same:

"Unknown age, sex, address, unknown causes, found at 8213 W. Summerdale Avenue, unincorporated section of Norwood Park Township."

Today, the authorities made their first identification of a victim. They said that a skeleton found under the garage was that of John Butkovich, 18 years old, of west suburban Lombard. He was last seen on July 31, 1975, when he said he was going to Mr. Gacy's house to pick up a paycheck.

TOLD OF 32 KILLINGS

None of the other severely decomposed bodies has been identified yet. But each was somebody's child.

And any one of the thousands of young people who have been drifting across the face of America could eventually be identified as one of those in shallow graves under the modest brick-fronted house.

Investigators have said that Mr. Gacy told them he killed as many as 32 young men in the last four years, most of them by strangulation, after having sexual relations with them. A chubby 36-year-old remodeling contractor, Mr. Gacy is being held without bond in the medical wing of the Cook County Jail on charges that he murdered a missing 15-year-old Des Plaines boy. In the late 1960's, Mr. Gacy served 18 months in an Iowa State prison for sodomizing a teen-age boy.

Investigators have speculated that at least some of the bodies being dug from the home's crawl space are those of youthful transients, a few of the lonely legions who follow the sun to California, Arizona, Texas and Florida, or are drawn to the urban excitement of such high-rise cities as New York and Chicago.

'NOT GETTING THE VOLUME'

Sgt. Howard Anderson of the Cook County Sheriff's Department said that investigators had only eight or nine missing persons from this area who were considered possible victims in the case, leading them to believe that a number were from outside the region.

"We're getting calls, and we're getting stuff in the mail now," he said, "but we're just not getting the volume you'd expect. In the future, I would expect hundreds. Maybe it's because of what happened. If it was a bus accident, I guess they'd call, but since it's a homosexual thing, well ..."

Last year alone, 175,557 persons under the age of 18 were reported missing, according to the Federal Bureau of Investigation's uniform crime report, which is compiled from statistics provided by 9,582 police departments. In the same period, the Chicago police received 19,000 reports of missing youths. Neither figure has varied significantly in recent years.

There are a lot of young people — some runaways, some wanderers — who maintain tenuous contacts with home. They are not so visible now, almost everyone agrees, as in the late 60's and early 70's, when their long hair and their clothes set them apart as hippies, street people and Vietnam War protesters. But they are there, scarcely noticed by the police or by anybody else; scarcely missed when they disappear, except by worried families.

And, as in the 1971 conviction of Juan V. Corona, a farm labor contractor, in the slaying and burial of 25 itinerant fruit pickers in California, it takes a lot of people dead in one place at one time to make society wonder how so many absences could go unnoticed for so long.

The Chicago police have come under some public criticism because they turned up nothing unusual in 1975 and 1976 when parents of two 17-year-old youths who had worked for Mr. Gacy reported their sons missing.

But Mike Gold. spokesman for the National Runaway Switchboard, a Chicago-based organization that maintains a 24-hour, toll-free line for youngsters who need advice or assistance, said: "As I recall, the police have stated that they have to give the younger kids priority, the 12-year-olds and younger, and that's the logical way of doing it."

Noting that his organization handles about 50,000 calls a year, most of them anonymously at the youngsters' request, Mr. Gold added: "It's a very, very difficult situation for the police department. If a kid is going to run away, he's not going to be found very easily by the police. It's too easy for the kids to submerge. The good news is that most runaways return home within three or four weeks, and a great many return home within a couple of days."

David M. Mozee, a spokesman for the Chicago Police Department, agreed.

"It's a monumental problem," he said. "We investigate every one we can. The younger the child, the more intensive the investigation. We can't do anything to a 17-year-old runaway. All we can do, if we see the kid, is tell the parents we've seen him."

As for the two missing youths who once worked for Mr. Gacy, Mr. Mozee said that he was not familiar with the details of the investigation into the disappearance of Gregory Godzik, who was last seen two years ago, but that he had seen reports on the case of John Butkovich.

"We talked to a lot of his friends, and we talked to Gacy," Mr. Mozee said of the Butkovich case. "But there were no leads. We questioned Gacy, we followed Gacy, but we found nothing wrong. We knew of the conviction in Iowa, but that doesn't make him a mass killer."

Mr. Mozee described the recent arrest of Mr. Gacy and the discovery of the bodies at the contractor's home as "a fluke, because a Des Plaines lieutenant had a 15-year-old boy."

Lieut. Joseph Kozenczak, chief of detectives in suburban Des Plaines, conceded that the fact that he had a son the same age and in the same high school with Robert Piest, the 15-year-old who disappeared on Dec. 11, made him pursue that case with more diligence than usual.

The Piest boy was reported missing after he left his job at a pharmacy, where Mr. Gacy had been doing some remodeling work, after telling his mother that he had to talk with a contractor about a promised summer job.

CHARGED WITH BOY'S MURDER

After following Mr. Gacy for several days and searching his home — the police said they found evidence that the Piest youth had been there — the Des Plaines police charged the contractor with the boy's murder. Mr. Gacy is reported to have told investigators that he threw the Piest boy's body into the Des Plaines River and disposed of four or five other bodies the same way.

After Mr. Gacy told the police a rambling tale about the bodies buried on his property, investigators said, a search of Mr. Gacy's home was begun.

Officials said that so far they had received 15 sets of dental charts from parents who thought their missing sons might have been among the victims. The officials asked concerned parents around the country to send any information that might help in determining the names of those uncovered.

While the dread of knowing what is now only a possibility might affect parents of missing persons everywhere, it weighed especially heavily on the families of John Butkovich and Gregory Godzik. Investigators reported finding wallets containing identification of both youths in Mr. Gacy's home.

There was a bleakness close to despair in the homes of both families this Christmas season.

Before his son's body was identified, Marko Butkovich said that after years of hearing little about the progress of the Chicago police investigation into the disappearance of his son, a youth officer told him: "If he is dead, we'll find him, but if he's not, then there's nothing we can do."

At the Godzik home on the Northwest Side, Eugenia Godzik recalled the last time she had seen her son on Dec. 11, 1976.

"We were going to church, and he sat down with a jar of cookies and milk," she said. "He was real excited because he was going out with a young lady he'd had his eye on for a long time. When he wasn't in his room the next morning, we called her and she said he let her off around 12:30. So we contacted all his friends. And they didn't know where he was."

She said that her son had liked his new employer, for whom he had worked only five or six weeks. "I don't think anybody thought anything about Gacy" in connection with her son's disappearance, she said.

As the search in Norwood Park Township goes on. Gregory Godzik is still missing. In a closet at his home, there are unopened presents waiting — presents from three Christmases past.

Suspect in Mass Deaths Is Puzzle to All

BY DOUGLAS E. KNEELAND | JAN. 10, 1979

CHICAGO, JAN. 9 — In the clean, well-lighted world of middle-class America, the hard-working, outgoing, community-spirited man next door is not supposed to be the suspect in the worst instance of mass killings in the United States in this century.

But John Wayne Gacy is that.

Tomorrow, Mr. Gacy, a short, round, 36-year-old remodeling contractor, is scheduled to appear in a Cook County courtroom for arraignment in a case that may ultimately involve the deaths of at least 32 young men in the last several years. A grand jury has indicted him in seven murders and the prosecutors are seeking further indictments as more of the 29 bodies recovered so far are identified.

But who is John Wayne Gacy?

AFFABLE, DRIVEN BUSINESSMAN

Is he the affable businessman, driven, often boastful, but as eager to please as a puppy? The clown, Pogo, who entertained children at picnics and parties? The outgoing man most neighbors, friends and family members knew here, in Springfield, Ill., and in Waterloo, Iowa?

Or is he the night wanderer portrayed by investigators, a man who cruised the homosexual scene's meanest streets in his late model black Oldsmobile with police-like spotlights, picking up young male prostitutes or other willing partners? The man who lured youngsters into his contracting business, brutalized them sexually and killed them? The unreformed former convict who served 18 months in an Iowa reformatory after he was convicted in 1968 of having engaged a Waterloo teen-ager in sodomy?

Or is he both?

A close look at his past does not provide easy answers as to why and at what point John Gacy's life may have taken the turn that made him the prime suspect in the bizarre sex murders. Most people who knew him will not discuss him, and those who will seem confused by the charges against him. But a look at Mr. Gacy's life does provide a picture, puzzling, perhaps even troubling, in its contradictions, of the man who sits quietly in the hospital wing of the Cook County Jail awaiting tomorrow's proceedings.

John Wayne Gacy was born in Edgewater Hospital here on March 17, 1942. His parents were John and Marian Gacy, both factory workers, and he grew up with his sisters, one two years older and one two years younger, in a working-class neighborhood on the northwest side. His father died nine years ago and his mother, who is 71 years old, lives with his younger sister in Arkansas. The elder sister lives in Chicago.

All three family members have desperately sought anonymity. But his younger sister, an articulate, sandy-haired mother of three, agreed to an interview if her identity was not disclosed.

'JUST A NORMAL PERSON'

"He was a normal person like everyone else," she said, "just a normal person. My mother just can't believe it. All she does is cry. I hope people know we're being torn apart by this. We just can't accept it yet."

The only unusual thing that she could recall about her brother's younger years, she said, was that he occasionally had blackouts. The problem, she continued, was diagnosed when he was 16 as a blood clot on the brain that was thought to have resulted from a playground accident five years earlier. He was treated and apparently cured, she said.

John Gacy went to Cooley Vocational High School, where he took business courses, his sister said. After a year, he transferred to Prosser Vocational High School, then dropped out after a couple of months. Later, he attended Northwestern Business College of Chicago.

VISITED ONCE OR TWICE YEARLY

With tears clouding her eyes, Mr. Gacy's sister said that he had always been the sort of brother and son who could not do enough for his family, who stayed in close touch by telephone and who visited once or twice a year.

The family knew of his sodomy conviction in Iowa, she said, but considered it "an incident in his life that he paid for."

Turning to happier memories, such as her brother's penchant for playing Pogo in clown costumes he had designed for himself, she said that he had always enjoyed entertaining children.

In 1964, shortly before he turned 22, Mr. Gacy, who had been hired by the Nunn-Bush Shoe Company here, was transferred to Springfield as manager of the concern's retail outlet at Roberts Brothers, a men's clothing store.

MARRIED SPRINGFIELD CO-WORKER

There he met Marlynn Myers, who also worked at the store. They were married nine months later and moved into the home left behind by his wife's parents, who had purchased a string of Kentucky Fried Chicken franchises in Waterloo.

In Springfield, Mr. Gacy plunged furiously into his job and into community life, joining the Jaycees, a service club. He was elected first vice president and chosen as the chapter's outstanding man of the year in 1965.

"He was a very bright person, energetic and never displayed any abnormal signs," recalled Ed McCreight, who worked with Mr. Gacy in the Springfield Jaycees.

The only incident Mr. McCreight said he remembered as being at all unusual came when he and Mr. Gacy were working on a parade route and Mr. Gacy put a flashing red light on the dashboard of his car.

TOLD NOT TO USE LIGHTS

"I asked him what he was doing," Mr. McCreight said. "He said, 'I've got a card that says I'm entitled to it.' I told him he might be entitled to it in Chicago, but not to use it here."

Mr. Gacy's former father in law, Fred W. Myers, sold his fried-chicken franchises in Waterloo a year and a half ago and moved back to Springfield. Speaking hesitantly through the door of his home, open a crack, Mr. Myers said, "I can't understand why they would have let him out of prison in Iowa."

In 1966, the Gacys moved to Waterloo, where he helped Mr. Myers manage the fast-food outlets. Mr. Gacy again threw himself into Jay-cees' activities. In 1967, he was vice president of the Waterloo Jaycees, chaplain of the chapter and chairman of its prayer breakfast.

'A REAL GO-GETTER'

"He was a real go-getter," said Charles Hill, manager of a Waterloo motel and a friend of Mr. Gacy. "He did a good job and was an excellent Jaycee."

Some others were not as receptive to Mr. Gacy's outgoing ways.

"He was a glad-hander type who would go beyond that," said Tom Langlas, a lawyer who knew Mr. Gacy through the Jaycees. "He'd shower too much attention on you as a way of getting more attention himself."

And Peter Burk, a lawyer who opposed Mr. Gacy in 1968 for the local Jaycees presidency, which he subsequently won after Mr. Gacy was charged in the sodomy case, said: "He was not a man tempered by truth. He seemed unaffected when caught in lies."

In May 1968 two teen-age boys told a Black Hawk County grand jury that Mr. Gacy had forced them to commit sexual acts with him.

YOUTH SAID GACY CHAINED HIM

According to the grand jury records, one of the youths said that Mr. Gacy had chained him and had begun choking him, but that when he stopped resisting his assailant loosened the chains and allowed him to leave.

He was indicted, convicted and sentenced, in December 1968, to 10 years at the state reformatory at Anamosa.

While he was in the reformatory, on Sept. 18, 1969, his wife, Marlynn, was granted a divorce on the ground of cruel and inhuman treatment and was given custody of their children.

Now remarried, she was reticent about discussing her past with Mr. Gacy, but agreed to an interview if her new name was not divulged.

Although she said she had not seen Mr. Gacy for more than nine years, she expressed shock at the murder charges.

"I just couldn't believe it," she said. "I never had any fear of him. It's hard for me to relate to these killings. I was never afraid of him."

NO SIGNS OF HOMOSEXUALITY

She said that she had "problems believing that he was homosexual" at the time of the Iowa sodomy indictment. She said nothing in their married life had indicated that.

She added that he had never been violent and that he had been a good father.

While Mr. Gacy's sister had described their family as extremely close, his former wife said cryptically that if he had developed any sort of mental problems they might have stemmed from his relationship with his father.

She declined to explain, except to say: "He and his dad did not get along. They were never close."

At the reformatory in Anamosa, Mr. Gacy is remembered as a model prisoner who headed the Jaycees chapter, worked in the kitchen and was paroled after 18 months.

'GOOD WORKER' IN REFORMATORY

"He had no particular problem during his stay," said Warden Calvin Auger. "His adjustment was exceptionally good. He was a good worker, a willing worker with only one minor disciplinary thing on his record, just a hassle with another resident with nobody injured."

He also said that there had been no evidence of homosexual activity on Mr. Gacy's part while he was in the reformatory.

One source who was familiar with a report on Mr. Gacy by an Iowa City psychiatrist before the sentence for sodomy said that the doctor had concluded that Mr. Gacy exhibited anti-social tendencies that could not be medically cured.

NOTHING ABNORMAL IN EXAM

However, Mr. Auger said that a routine psychological examination of Mr. Gacy when he entered the reformatory "didn't show anything that abnormal."

In Des Moines, Donald L. Olson, executive secretary of the Iowa State Board of Parole, which released Mr. Gacy from prison on June 18, 1970, said that the contents of Mr. Gacy's file were privileged.

"There are psychiatric reports," he added. "But I can tell you this: If there were any red flags, he wouldn't have been paroled."

When Mr. Gacy left the reformatory, he returned to Chicago, where he worked at a restaurant and lived with his mother. After about four months in an apartment on the northwest side, he is reported to have borrowed money from his mother to buy his house at 8213 West Summerdale Avenue in Norwood Park Township.

Later, he started his own business, P.D.M. (for painting, decorating and maintenance) Contractors, which he operated out of his home. He specialized in doing remodeling work at retail stores and subcontracted work on larger construction projects.

YOUTHS SAID THEY REBUFFED HIM

Over the years, he hired a succession of youths to work with him. The bodies of two have been identified from among those discovered at his home. Since his arrest, others who worked for him have said that he made sexual overtures toward them, but that they had rebuffed him and he had laughed the matter off.

Although Mr. Gacy was released from parole Oct. 19, 1971, he had been arrested on Feb. 12, 1971, according to police records, after a teenager complained that Mr. Gacy had picked him up in a bus station and tried to force him to commit a sexual act. The charge was dismissed when the boy did not appear in court.

There is no record as to whether the incident was ever brought to the attention of Mr. Gacy's parole officer.

Meanwhile, the Chicago police have acknowledged that they staked out Mr. Gacy's home for two weeks in January 1976, when a 9-year-old boy prostitute was missing. The police said they questioned a number of young men going in and out of the Gacy home, but none would say anything against him.

NO LINKS FOUND TO GACY

The police also investigated, in 1975 and in 1976, the separate disappearances of the two youths who had worked for him, but did not turn up anything linking Mr. Gacy to them.

On Dec. 31, 1977, a 19-year-old man charged that Mr. Gacy had kidnapped him at gunpoint and forced him to commit sexual acts, but no criminal charges were filed, according to the police records. The officials said that Mr. Gacy had acknowledged the acts, but had said the man was a willing participant who later tried to blackmail him.

Last March, another young man accused Mr. Gacy of having abducted, chloroformed and raped him. A misdemeanor charge of battery is still pending.

"When these things come up, people say the police should have come up with a pattern," said David M. Mozee, a spokesman for the police, "but we have a good conscience. We questioned Gacy, we followed Gacy, but we found nothing wrong. We knew of the conviction in Iowa, but that doesn't make him a mass killer."

All the while, to his neighbors in Norwood Park Township, he was just the man next door, a trustee of the township's street lighting district, a Democratic precinct captain, a fun-loving person who gave parties for as many as 400 friends and then shared the leftover liquor and food with those who lived nearby.

In June 1972, Mr. Gacy married Carole Hoff, a divorced woman with two daughters.

"He swept me off my feet," she said.

Then one time, she said, she found several wallets apparently belonging to teen-age boys in his car. He exploded in anger.

"He would throw furniture," she said. "He broke a lot of my furniture. I think now, if there were murders, some must have taken place when I was in that house."

The couple was divorced March 2, 1976.

She has said recently on television that he was sexually dysfunctional with women.

Even when he was being followed openly by the Des Plaines police shortly before he was arrested and charged with murder, Mr. Gacy's neighbors could not believe what was happening.

Sam and Jennie DeLaurentis, who lived across the street, recalled that they had asked him why the police cars were following him all the time. They said he told them that the police were "trying to pin a murder rap on me." They said he laughed and they laughed.

That was before the police found evidence at Mr. Gacy's home that Robert Piest, a 15-year-old who disappeared after going to see him on Dec. 11 about a summer job, had been there. The contractor is reported to have told the authorities that he threw the youth's body into the Des Plaines River.

Since they began digging three days before Christmas, Cook County sheriff's investigators have dug up 27 decomposed bodies from under Mr. Gacy's garage and modest three-bedroom ranch house.

The authorities have said that Mr. Gacy has told them that he killed 32 youths after having sexual relations with them, burying 27 at this home and throwing the bodies of five into the Des Plaines River.

Two bodies have been recovered from the river, making the 29 linked to the case so far the largest number of victims attributed to a murder suspect in the United States in this century, at least.

"He was a kind, friendly and generous neighbor," Lillie Grexa said. "We were close neighbors. Our house was open to him and his was open to us. I still can't believe how John could have done that."

Suspect Pleads Not Guilty to 7 Murder Counts at Hearing on Sex Attacks

BY DOUGLAS E. KNEELAND | JAN. 11, 1979

CHICAGO, JAN. 10 — John Wayne Gacy stood quietly in a heavily guarded Cook County courtroom here today as his lawyer entered a not guilty plea for him in seven murder indictments.

At the arraignment proceedings, which lasted about an hour and a half, Mr. Gacy remained silent, his hands clasped at his waist, his head bowed slightly, only occasionally glancing over his right shoulder toward the bullet-proof glass wall that separated him from the spectators' seats.

Light from courtroom's windows reflected on the glass wall, preventing Mr. Gacy from catching more than a blurred glimpse of the 85 persons who filled all the available public seats. Among the spectators were Harold and Elizabeth Piest of Des Plaines, the parents of 15-year-old Robert Piest, one of the alleged victims.

The short, chubby remodeling contractor, who is 36 years old, was arrested three days before Christmas and charged with the murder of Robert Piest, who had been missing since Dec. 11. Subsequently, investigators said, he told them he had killed the youth and 31 others, after having had sexual relations with them, burying 27 at his home and throwing the bodies of five others into the Des Plaines River.

27 BODIES RECOVERED

Sheriff's investigators have recovered 27 bodies from beneath Mr. Gacy's home and garage in Norwood Park Township, suburb of Chicago. Two bodies found in the river also have been linked to Mr. Gacy by evidence discovered at his home, the authorities said.

A county grand jury is still hearing evidence in the case, but on Monday handed up indictments charging Mr. Gacy with murder in the deaths of Robert Piest, whose body has not been found, and of six of the 10 other victims whose remains have been identified.

On Dec. 29, Mr. Gacy had been scheduled for a preliminary hearing at county courthouse in Des Plaines, but Chief Judge Richard J. Fitzgerald ordered a delay and rescheduled the proceedings, for security reasons, for the Criminal Courts Building in Chicago. The old courthouse is connected by a tunnel with the hospital wing of Cook County Jail, where the prisoner is being held.

Today, Mr. Gacy was brought through the tunnel and then up to the fourth-floor courtroom by a route that kept him from public view until, with four sheriff's deputies close behind, he walked to the bench with his attorneys.

Twenty news people were allowed in the jury box of the courtroom, which was remodeled for special security cases in 1973. Mr. Gacy wearing a brown jacket and tie and beige pants that dragged slightly on the floor, did not look at them as he entered. Later, as he left for a brief recess, he half lifted his left hand in a gesture toward the jury box and when he returned, he nodded twice, smiling slightly, as if he thought he recognized someone there.

Otherwise, Mr. Gacy appeared to be expressionless as the indictments were read and as one of his lawyers, Sam Amirante, filed a series of motions. Mr. Amirante urged that the charges be dismissed because of pretrial, and pre-indictment publicity, that the search at Mr. Gacy's home be halted and that Mr. Gacy undergo a psychiatric examination.

Gacy Is Found Guilty of Killing 33, Record for U.S. Mass Murder

BY NATHANIEL SHEPPARD JR. | MARCH 13, 1980

CHICAGO, MARCH 12 — John Wayne Gacy was found guilty today of 33 murders, more than any other mass killer in the history of the nation.

The jury of seven men and five women reached the verdict after less than two hours of deliberation, indicating that it was unswayed by defense assertions that the 37-year-old building contractor was mentally ill and not responsible for the crimes. The jurors are to hear arguments tomorrow on whether he should be sentenced to die in the electric chair.

The verdict followed 23 days of emotionally charged testimony in the trial, which began more than a year after a young man's body was found in a crawl space under Mr. Gacy's home in suburban Northwood Township. More bodies were found, and Mr. Gacy was eventually charged with murdering 33 boys and young men lured to his home with the promise of jobs, but for the purpose of sex, from 1972 to 1978.

Mr. Gacy was also convicted of deviate sexual assault and of taking indecent liberties with a minor — 15-year-old Robert Piest, whose disappearance more than two years ago led to Mr. Gacy's arrest.

Mr. Gacy was arrested Dec. 22, 1978, and charged with murdering the Piest youth, whom prosecutors said was his last victim. He subsequently told investigators of committing other murders.

Twenty-eight bodies were found in the crawl space, another beneath Mr. Gacy's garage, and four more in the Des Plaines River. Eleven remain unidentified.

Terry Sullivan, an assistant state's attorney, said of the verdict, "We are very glad and I am very satisfied. The people of Illinois should be very satisfied that the jury returned a verdict" in such a short time.

Mr. Gacy's lawyers made no immediate comment, including whether an appeal would be filed. A death sentence is automatically appealed in Illinois.

At issue in the trial was not whether Mr. Gacy had committed the slayings; the evidence of his guilt was overwhelming and he had confessed on three ocassions. Instead, the arguments centered on whether Mr. Gacy was a cold-blooded murderer who had planned the killings, or a mentally diseased man who was incapable of understanding his actions.

The 108 witnesses included relatives and friends of Mr. Gacy who described him as the product of a tortured childhood, defense psychiatrists who described him as psychologically incompetent, and prosecution psychiatrists who said he was well aware of his actions.

Mr. Gacy at one point told Judge Louis B. Garippo that he had resisted an insanity defense, but later said he did not understand the proceedings.

The prosecutors painstakingly reconstructed the gruesome details of how Mr. Gacy lured his victims to his home with the promise of high-paying jobs, engaged in sex with them, then killed them, most by strangulation.

'EVIL, VILE AND DIABOLICAL MAN'

In closing arguments yesterday Mr. Sullivan spent more than three hours dramatically detailing 23 of the killings. He described Mr. Gacy as "an evil, vile and diabolical man, a sadistic animal" who had "snuffed out 33 lives like they were candles,"

In his closing arguments Sam Amirante, Mr. Gacy's attorney, compared his client to Edward Hyde, the alter-ego of Dr. Henry Jeykll in the Robert Louis Stevenson story.

"John Gacy is a madman who has been reaching out, saying, 'Stop me before I kill again,' " Mr. Amirante said.

Mr. Amirante pleaded with the jurors to find Mr. Gacy not guilty by reason of insanity, to "take the first step to have him studied, to try to prevent something like this from happening again."

WEPT AS EX-WIFE TESTIFIED

Throughout most of the trial Mr. Gacy sat expressionless, often with relatives of the victims sobbing a short distance behind him. But when his former wife, Carol Lofgren, testified that she felt sorry for him, both of them wept.

Mrs. Lofgren testified that at the beginning of their marriage they had normal sexual relations, although he had told her he was bisexual.

Until today, the largest mass-murder conviction in the nation's history was that of Juan V. Corona, found guilty in 1972 of killing 25 itinerant farm workers in California and now awaiting retrial. Because of extensive publicity given the Gacy case, the jurors were selected in Winnebago County, some 70 miles away, and brought here for the trial.

Kenneth Piest, a brother of the youth whose disappearance led to Mr. Gacy's arrest, said he had attended all but a few days of the trial and that this had helped him deal with the shock of his younger brother's murder.

"For the first time in 15 months I am happy," he said outside the courtroom today. "But the case is not over — none of us will be satisfied until he's put to death."

Mrs. Eugenia Godzik, the mother of another victim, said:

"He's got to get the chair. All of us mothers — we paid for those lives. He should get the death penalty."

Man Who Killed 33 Is Executed in Illinois

BY JOHN KIFNER | MAY 10, 1994

JOHN WAYNE GACY, convicted 14 years ago of the sex-related killings of 33 young men and boys, was put to death by lethal injection early today as the nation's worst serial killer on record.

The execution, which took place in the old Stateville penitentiary here, followed last-minute appeals filed by Mr. Gacy's lawyers, asserting that their 52-year-old client was mentally incompetent, that he was out of town at the time of 16 of the slayings and that Illinois' method of execution was unconstitutional.

But none of the state or Federal judges appealed to on Monday, including Justice John Paul Stevens of the United States Supreme Court, would stay Mr. Gacy's execution.

Howard A. Peters, a corrections official, said Mr. Gacy was pronounced dead at 12:58 P.M., nearly an hour after the injection of three lethal chemicals had been scheduled to begin. The process was delayed because gelling prevented the chemicals from flowing through a delivery tube, Mr. Peters said. The prisoner gave a final statement proclaiming his innocence, Mr. Peters said.

DEMONSTRATIONS PRO AND CON

Mr. Gacy inspired a range of emotions and passions since the first of his victims was discovered beneath his Chicago house. And yesterday it was all the more so. Opponents of capital punishment gathered in Chicago to urge that Mr. Gacy's life be spared, as others, like the Guardian Angels anti-crime group, gathered in Chicago to demand that his execution be carried out.

Although the authorities said Mr. Gacy had at one time confessed, he later insisted he was innocent, even going so far as to state his case

Some of the 5,000 demonstrators supporting the scheduled execution of serial killer John Wayne Gacy hold balloons and wear party hats as they march in a Gacy Day Parade on May 9, 1994, in Chicago.

in a recording that the public could hear via a 900 telephone number. But the authorities said the evidence of his guilt was overwhelming.

Mr. Gacy, an ordinary-seeming businessman who had dressed as a clown to entertain children, had served as a Democratic Party precinct captain and had organized annual celebrations of Polish holidays attracting hundreds of people, was convicted in March 1980 of murdering 33 boys and young men between 1972 and 1978. All but six of his victims were found buried beneath his house.

'YOU JUST CAN'T TELL'

"It wasn't like he had horns, or a sign," Michael Albrecht, who shadowed, then arrested, Mr. Gacy said on Monday on one of the many radio talk shows in the Chicago area that were dominated by Mr. Gacy's pending execution. "He was very popular, very well-liked. You just can't tell."

Although even one of Mr. Gacy's defense lawyers has been quoted as calling him a "poster child for the death penalty," opponents of capital punishment argued that even he should not be executed.

"It's an American tragedy that we're doing this," Jay Miller of the American Civil Liberties Union said at a news conference on Monday called by a coalition opposing the death penalty. "This is shocking that in our name we are going to kill another person. No matter what that person did, we're setting a terrible example that human life is really not worth it."

On Monday morning, Mr. Gacy was taken under tight security from the downstate Menard Correctional Center, where he had spent the last 14 years, and was flown by helicopter to the penitentiary here. He was put in a 7-by-9-foot cell in a one-story structure called Building X, which had been cleared of its 40 inmates. A guard was posted opposite his cell door on a suicide watch, although his lawyers said he has never showed any signs of distress or remorse.

Mr. Howell, the prisons spokesman said: "He was very chatty. He was talking up a storm." He said Mr. Gacy had discussed with his guards, among other things, the prospects of the Chicago Cubs.

For a last meal, prison officials said, Mr. Gacy asked for fried chicken, fried shrimp, french fries and fresh strawberries. A spokesman for the Illinois Department of Correction, Nic Howell, said Mr. Gacy had said he especially enjoyed the shrimp.

TRICKED INTO DEATH

The case gripped the public at the end of 1978, when the police began digging up body after body from a crawl space under Mr. Gacy's modest but comfortable suburban home near O'Hare International Airport.

Eventually 27 bodies were found under the house; 2 others were found elsewhere on the property, apparently buried there when Mr. Gacy ran out of room in the crawl space, and 4 more were found dumped in the Des Plaines River.

A jury concluded that the victims, lured to the house for sex, were killed from 1972 to 1978. Usually they were tricked into allowing a rope, twisted tight with a stick, to be tied around their necks.

Only 25 victims have been identified; the others were buried in charity funerals under gravestones that said only, "We Are Remembered."

As an inmate on Death Row, Mr. Gacy took up art. In a macabre twist, the crude paintings of his Pogo the Clown character and other cartoonish works he churned out in his windowless cell at the Menard Correctional Center now command as much as $20,000 apiece from collectors. Mr. Gacy received more mail — and methodically answered it — than any other inmate at the prison, and for $23.88 callers could dial a 900 line and, for 12 minutes, listen to his soft voice denying the crimes.

CLOWNS AND SKULLS

On Monday, a downtown Chicago art gallery had a show of more than 60 of Mr. Gacy's oil paintings and sketches. One of the paintings, never before displayed, depicts a chair with a clown costume draped over it; others feature skulls and the Crucifixion.

Jim Rider, the assistant curator of the Canal Street Gallery, said Mr. Gacy preferred to paint happier scenes, including Disney-like representations of the Seven Dwarfs, but turned to the grimmer scenes because "he recognizes the market."

"People come and are fascinated by the fact that these are the artistic efforts of a man who also killed 33 people," Mr. Rider said.

CHAPTER 5

Jeffrey Dahmer

Clean-cut and easy-going much of the time, Jeffrey
Dahmer also had dark inclinations. As a child he killed
small animals, impaling them and displaying their skeletons on trees. He craved attention, disrupting classes and
pulling pranks in high school. Dahmer drank heavily and
mocked the people around him. And he killed people. He
drugged, strangled and butchered at least 15 teenage
boys and young men. He had sex with his dead victims. He
ate parts of their bodies. He was a nightmare come true.

Milwaukee Police Once Queried Suspect

BY JAMES BARRON | JULY 27, 1991

TWO MONTHS BEFORE butchered bodies were discovered in Jeffrey L.
Dahmer's apartment in Milwaukee, neighbors called the police and
said they had seen a dazed-looking teen-ager shambling on the street
outside, naked and bleeding.

The police who investigated left after Mr. Dahmer apparently persuaded them that the young man was of age, that the two were living
together and that the incident was a domestic dispute.

The teen-ager, identified by the authorities as Konerak Sinthasomphone, 14 years old, is now dead, one of as many as 11 victims found in
the second-floor apartment that neighbors said was known throughout the complex for foul smells and the whine of an electric saw. The
dead youth was the brother of another teen-aged boy Mr. Dahmer was

convicted of molesting two years ago, a crime for which he was on probation before his arrest this week.

THREE OFFICERS ARE SUSPENDED

Yesterday the three police officers who spoke with Mr. Dahmer at his apartment in May were suspended with pay.

"There is no doubt I am taken aback by this information," Chief of Police Philip Arreola said at a news conference, according to The Associated Press. "This is a matter of grave concern to me and the entire department."

Chief Arreola said the officers were suspended because they did not write a formal report or run Mr. Dahmer's name through the police computer, which would have revealed his prior child-molestation conviction. He said he would take whatever action was warranted once the investigation was completed.

The neighbors who sought help at the time say the officers brushed off their complaint. They said Mr. Dahmer emerged from his apartment and chatted with the officers. Then they let the teen-ager, who was muttering and incoherent, which Mr. Dahmer explained as the result of drinking, go back inside with him. That was on May 27. Konerak Sinthasomphone has been missing since the day before, The A.P. reported.

"This could have all been prevented," Nicole Childress, 18, one of the women who called the police, was quoted as saying. "If they had listened that night, that little boy would still be alive and all the others wouldn't be dead."

The boy and his brother, who was molested by Mr. Dahmer when he was 13, were both members of a family of refugees from Laos.

Ms. Childress and a cousin were quoted by The Associated Press as saying they saw a boy, bleeding from his buttocks, on the street near Mr. Dahmer's apartment. But a police spokesman, Capt. Joseph Purpero, said, "The information we have is he was bleeding from a skinned knee."

Mr. Dahmer, 31, has been charged with four murders and the police say they plan more charges. The former candy factory worker, who lost his job a week ago and told the authorities he was deeply in debt and facing eviction on Aug. 1, has acknowledged drugging, strangling and dismembering 11 people there. He is said to have boiled some skulls to remove the flesh and to have kept one heart in a freezer to eat later.

The identities of three more victims were disclosed yesterday: Erroll Lindsey, 19, Curtis Straughter, 18, and Ernest Miller, 22, all of Milwaukee. One of the 11 victims has yet to be identified.

FAMILY'S DOUBLE TRAGEDY

On the night police officers were called to Mr. Dahmer's apartment, he apparently persuaded them that he and the Sinthasomphone youth were living together and had been drinking. The officers were said to have listed the incident as a "domestic squabble between homosexuals."

But Ms. Childress said of the youth, "He was struggling; he was reaching out to me for help." The other woman, Sandra Smith, 18, said: "We tried to give the policemen our names, but he just told us to butt out."

Chief Arreola said there was no indication that the Sinthasomphone killing was in retaliation for Mr. Dahmer's sexual assault conviction involving the victim's brother, for which Mr. Dahmer was given a 10-month sentence. He is said to have lured the brother, then 13, to his apartment with an offer of $50 to pose for pictures.

INVESTIGATION IN OHIO

The two incidents struck a family that found its way to Milwaukee in 1980, after fleeing the Communist regime of Laos, Laotian residents in Milwaukee told The A.P. "It is like you are running and you think you escape but you are coming to a dangerous world in this place," said Shoua Xiong, executive director of the Lao Family Community Inc.

Anoukone Sinthasomphone, the 25-year-old brother of the two boys, told The A.P. yesterday: "We thought it likely that he was in there. The whole thing is crazy. It is terrible."

Mr. Dahmer has also told Milwaukee detectives that he committed a murder in Ohio in 1978, the year he graduated from high school there. Yesterday the authorities in Bath, Ohio, the town near Akron where Mr. Dahmer grew up, began preparing to dig up the yard outside the house where his family lived and to search the woods nearby. The Dahmers moved some years ago.

Detectives from the Summit County Sheriff's Department and the Bath police interviewed Mr. Dahmer in Milwaukee yesterday, and there may be further questioning today.

The authorities have refused to identify the missing person except to say that he was a 19-year-old male from Coventry, Ohio, about 15 miles from Bath. Mr. Dahmer is believed to have met him at a bar in Akron.

The complaint filed against Mr. Dahmer in Milwaukee said he took part in homosexual acts with at least three of the victims, including one who was already dead.

The police in Milwaukee say Mr. Dahmer brought men home from bars frequented by homosexuals and from shopping centers, promising them money if they would let him photograph them. Reuters quoted officials as saying that he often traveled to Chicago to seek out potential victims; he said he met one victim at a parade for homosexuals there.

Investigators are also looking into whether Mr. Dahmer may have been responsible for murders that remain unsolved in several other states and in Germany, where he was stationed as an Army medical orderly in Bad Kreuznach in the late 1970's and early 1980's.

17 Killed, and a Life
Is Searched for Clues

BY JAMES BARRON WITH MARY B. W. TABOR | AUG. 4, 1991

ON PAGE 98 OF Jeffrey L. Dahmer's Ohio high-school yearbook is a photograph of 45 honor society students lined up shoulder to shoulder, their hair well combed, their smiles confident.

One senior three rows from the top has no smile, no eyes, no face at all: his image was blacked out with a marking pen, reduced to a silhouette by an annoyed student editor before the yearbook went to the printer.

That silhouette was Mr. Dahmer in the spring of 1978, a couple of months before he says he killed his first victim, with a barbell. It was 13 years before he confessed to one of the most horrific strings of slayings in modern times.

With grades that ranged from A's to D's, Mr. Dahmer fell far short of honor society standards, but he sneaked into the photo session as if he belonged. No one said a word until long after the shutter had clicked.

In all the years he cried out for attention, it was one of the few times he got caught. By then he had taught himself to live behind a mask of normalcy that hid his often contradictory emotions. It was a mask no one pulled down until one night last month, when a man in handcuffs dashed out of Mr. Dahmer's bizarrely cluttered apartment in a tough Milwaukee neighborhood, called the police and stammered that Mr. Dahmer had been trying to kill him.

The authorities say that at least 17 other men did not get away; that Mr. Dahmer drugged their drinks, strangled them and cut up their bodies with an electric buzz saw; that he discarded bones he did not want in a 57-gallon drum he had bought for just that purpose; that he lined up three skulls on a shelf in his apartment, but only after spraying them with gray paint, to fool people into thinking that they were plastic models, the kind an aspiring artist or a medical intern might study.

Once, he told the police in Milwaukee, he fried a victim's bicep in vegetable shortening and ate it.

Some criminal psychologists see traits in Mr. Dahmer that they have studied in mass killers like Theodore Bundy, who was was electrocuted in Florida in 1989 after a 15-year trail of violence that investigators believe took the lives of at least 30 young women across the nation, or John Wayne Gacy, who was convicted in 1980 of the sex killings of 33 young men in Chicago.

"We're dealing with some of the same dynamics that we can see in Gacy: the dysfunctional family, a guy who denies his homosexual feelings to erase whatever shame he might feel in committing these acts, who destroys the people who attracted him in the first place," said Ted Cahill, who wrote a book about the Gacy killings. "He's punishing himself and punishing them at the same time."

Now everyone from detectives to radio talk-show hosts is puzzling over the Dahmer case. The facts by themselves — a home where parents went through a bitter divorce; a brother he long believed was the favorite in the family; a mother who he told the police had a nervous breakdown; his own lack of close friends — do not explain why he did what he says he did. But the increasingly gruesome details that have emerged about Mr. Dahmer have all led back to one basic question: Who is this man?

He was an elementary-school student who stored animal skeletons in bottles of formaldehyde. A high-school drinker who swigged Scotch in early morning classes. An Army medic who convinced his buddies that he hated anything more unpleasant than taking soldiers' blood pressure. A factory worker who killed a gay man in a Milwaukee hotel, packed the body into a suitcase, took an elevator to the lobby, hailed a cab and had the driver put the suitcase in the trunk.

Like Mr. Gacy and Mr. Bundy, Mr. Dahmer went undetected for years. Some of his victims came from the fringes of society, and there were so many that he could not remember them all — men he filed in his memory not by their names but by their tattoos. Some of them were like Mr. Dahmer himself, people of whom society did not take much notice.

And he could talk his way out of trouble when he had to. On May 27, nearly two months before his arrest, neighbors called the police about a naked, bleeding teen-ager they had seen wandering on the street outside Mr. Dahmer's apartment. The officers who investigated believed Mr. Dahmer's explanation that he and the boy were living together and were just having a quarrel.

After they left, Mr. Dahmer said later, he killed the teenager, Konerak Sinthasomphone. The officers have been suspended, with pay.

He had a glib side, talking his way into Vice President Walter F. Mondale's suite and the office of the humorist Art Buchwald on a school trip to Washington. But his hometown — Bath Township, Ohio, a prosperous community that was home to Firestones and other decision makers who presided over the tire factories of nearby Akron — was a tight-lipped place. Mr. Dahmer was tight-lipped about himself. And if anyone realized how unusual some of his behavior was, no one did anything about it.

"Whatever had gone on in Jeff's life, he couldn't talk about." said Martha Schmidt, a classmate at Revere High School who is now an assistant professor of sociology at Capital University in Columbus, Ohio. But she added, "It seemed so clear all along that it was someone saying, 'Pay attention to me.' "

He had been saying it for years. School records of his teachers' comments suggest that his feelings of alienation were apparent as early as first grade. His mother became ill in 1966 before and after the birth of his brother, David. "Jeff felt neglected," said a school official in Doylestown, Ohio, where Mr. Dahmer, then 6 years old, had been enrolled in Hazel Harvey Elementary School that fall.

The family moved to nearby Barberton before the school year was over, and a little more than a year later, when Mr. Dahmer was 8, they moved again, to Bath. From what his father, Lionel Dahmer, told a Milwaukee probation officer last year, that would have been about the time that Jeffrey Dahmer was sexually assaulted by a neighborhood boy. Jeffrey Dahmer, in his conversations with the police, has denied he was ever assaulted in that way.

Eric Tyson, who grew up across the street, said Jeffrey Dahmer kept chipmunk and squirrel skeletons in a backyard shed and had an animal burial ground at the side of the house, with graves and little crosses. "A number of neighbors have recalled seeing animals, like frogs and cats impaled, or staked to trees," he said.

Mr. Dahmer's high school record had the look of normalcy: he was in the band and played intramural tennis. But he drank. "I used to see him drinking gin," said Chip Crofoot, another classmate.

One day he went to a class with a Scotch, and Ms. Schmidt asked why he was drinking. "It's my medicine" was his reply, she said.

He sometimes tried to get attention by yelling odd exclamations in public places or by pretending to faint while crossing a street.

Sneaking into the honor society photograph became something of an annual prank: he did it when he was a junior as well as when he was a senior. "It was a very Jeff thing to do," Ms. Schmidt said. "It was part of his trying to be unconventional and to mock everything around him. I think he very consciously chose the honor society because I think in some ways he was laughing at himself and us."

TROUBLE AT HOME, AND THEN A KILLING

There was turbulence at home: the Dahmers' marriage was unraveling. One person who knew the Dahmers said that as things deteriorated Lionel Dahmer moved to a different part of the house to be away from his wife. He even jury-rigged an alarm, a string pulled across the room with keys hanging from it that would jangle if she intruded while he slept. Later Mr. Dahmer moved to a motel.

It was in the final weeks of the divorce settlement, just after Jeffrey Dahmer's high school graduation, that he says he committed his first homicide, a killing that went unreported until he told the police about it last month.

Mr. Dahmer told the police he picked up a hitchhiker named Steven Hicks and took him home for a beer. Mr. Dahmer said they had sex.

When Mr. Hicks wanted to leave, Mr. Dahmer smashed the back of his head with a barbell and then strangled him. He dragged the body into a crawlspace under the house, cut it into pieces and stored it in garbage bags. Later, he buried the bones, only to dig them up, crush them and scatter them in a ravine behind his parents' house.

That set a pattern that the authorities say Mr. Dahmer followed in Milwaukee, where he turned his grandmother's house and later his own apartment into killing factories. He would offer people a beer or money to pose in the nude while he took photographs. When they wanted to leave, he became violent.

SHOWING A DIFFERENT SIDE WHILE ON MILITARY DUTY

The next stop for Mr. Dahmer was Ohio State University, where he spent one semester. Then he enlisted in the Army and reported for duty at Fort McClellan, Ala., in the spring of 1980. He began training to be a military police officer, but soon transferred to Fort Sam Houston, in San Antonio, for a six-week course as a medical specialist, the military equivalent of a nurse's aide, a job that involved screening patients. He was assigned to the 2d Battalion, 68th Armored Regiment, 8th Infantry Division, and was sent to Baumholder in West Germany.

Mr. Dahmer decorated his room in Baumholder with a poster of the heavy-metal rock band Iron Maiden. He also spent hours poring over a children's picture book about the troll and the billy goats Gruff and telling boozy W. C. Fields jokes. Once he gave his bunkmate, Billy J. Capshaw, a birthday card with a beer mug on it and a Fields punchline. "To a fellow guzzler on his 19th birthday," he wrote on the card.

"He talked about his dad a lot," Mr. Capshaw said. "He wanted to please his dad." Mr. Capshaw believed that Mr. Dahmer was an only child. "He never said anything about a brother," Mr. Capshaw said last week.

Mr. Dahmer was clean-cut and easy-going, though he chided Mr. Capshaw for using foul language. But when he drank he became stony-faced and, to Mr. Capshaw, menacing.

"When he'd drink, he'd get real violent with me," said Mr. Capshaw, who is now serving a one-year sentence in the Garland County Jail in Hot Springs, Ark., for negligent homicide, a misdemeanor, involving a 14-year-old who borrowed his car and hit and killed someone. "You could tell in his face that he wasn't joking. It was for real. That's why it bothered me. It was a whole different side. His face was blank. It was kind of like he was cross-eyed-like. An expression like he just wasn't there. I've never seen it on anyone else's face."

KILLING BECOMES ALMOST A ROUTINE

Mr. Dahmer was honorably discharged in March 1981, a year before his three-year enlistment was over. The scuttlebutt around the barracks was that he was discharged for drinking. Army officials in Washington would not discuss the reasons, but Mr. Dahmer said he was discharged under Chapter 9 of the Code of Military Justice, a section that covers drug or alcohol use by Army personnel.

From what Mr. Dahmer told the police last month, fantasies of killing people that he had when he was 17 or 18 recurred after he left the Army and moved to Milwaukee, where his grandmother lived and where he eventually got a job at the Ambrosia Chocolate Company. But he told the police he did not kill again until late 1984 or early 1985, when he "discovered the gay bars."

Police reports written after his arrest last month said Mr. Dahmer met his first victim in Milwaukee at the 219 Club, a bar frequented by homosexuals. They went to the Ambassador Hotel, where a room for two costs $43.88 a night, plus a refundable $10 key deposit. In the police report he did not say he had killed the man; he just talked about how the two of them got drunk and passed out. "When he woke up, the guy was dead and had blood coming from his mouth," the report said, giving Mr. Dahmer's explanation of what happened next.

He told the police he left the body in the room while he went to a mall, bought a suitcase, returned to the hotel, put the body inside, called a taxi and took it to his grandmother's house, where he was living. There he dismembered the body and disposed of it. The police report did not say where his grandmother was at the time.

The police report said he did not kill his next victim until roughly a year later, this time at his grandmother's house. He told the police he met the man at the 219 Club and gave him sleeping pills after they had sex. Then he strangled the man after he dozed off. He said he also drugged his third victim at his grandmother's house.

TALKING OF EVERYTHING EXCEPT THE DARKEST SIDE

Mr. Dahmer was arrested in 1986 for taking photographs of a 14-year-old boy and was convicted and sentenced to a year in jail. The killings resumed, he told the police, when he was released after serving a partial sentence. He was seeing a parole officer at the same time.

He said that in 1989 he had sex with a man, drugged him and stabbed him with a hunting knife. Then he dismembered the body in the bathtub and used hydrochloric acid to destroy the bones.

Mr. Dahmer said his next killing, two months later, followed the same routine: sex, drugs in a drink, death and dismemberment. "Subject states he began getting quicker at cutting up the bodies," the police report noted.

What unfolded in his sessions with the parole-probation officer, Donna Chester, was a partial look at his life. She was unavailable for an interview last week. But her impressions of Mr. Dahmer recorded in an 81-page document that was released by the Wisconsin Department of Corrections, give no indication that Mr. Dahmer set off alarm bells during their chats.

The reason was that he seemed to talk about everything except the killings.

He sometimes expressed interest in talking about his sexual orientation, but often could not bring himself to say what was on his mind.

"Client states he knows he prefers male partners but client feels guilty about it." Ms. Chester wrote.

He also talked about family tensions. "He is uncomfortable with his family," she wrote after a session, "because (1) his father is controlling, (2) he has nothing in common with his brother who attends college and (3) he is embarrassed by his offense." He said he had talked with his mother and that she had told him she knew he was gay but that it did not matter.

Money was also on his mind. Ms. Chester wrote that Mr. Dahmer "gets angry at people who make a lot of money, saying "why are they so lucky?' And he 'hates' them for having so much."

Ms. Chester told Mr. Dahmer he had a good job, but he was frustrated that he always seemed short of cash and that the life he longed to lead was beyond his means. But for all of Mr. Dahmer's complaining about finances, his job appeared to be going well. He earned about $9 an hour at the candy factory and took home $250 to $300 a week, depending on how much overtime he put in.

Soon that security was in jeopardy. On July 8, Mr. Dahmer told Ms. Chester he was in danger of losing his job because of arriving late or not showing up.

On July 14, just days before his arrest, he told Ms. Chester he had been dismissed. He told her he had overslept after spending all day visiting his grandmother in a hospital.

The police reports indicate that the killings became more frequent as things at work deteriorated. He told the police that he killed on June 30, July 4 and July 19.

Three days after that last killing, he was arrested shortly after the man in handcuffs fled his apartment and flagged down police officers.

Clues to a Dark Nurturing Ground for One Serial Killer

BY DANIEL GOLEMAN | AUG 7, 1991

PERHAPS THE FIRST SIGN that something was seriously amiss with Jeffrey L. Dahmer came in 1975, when he was a teen-ager. A group of boys walking in the woods behind the Dahmer home found the head of a dog impaled on a stick, the police chief in Bath Township, Ohio, said recently.

The boys were so shocked at the sight that they took photographs, but they did not tell the police until Mr. Dahmer was arrested two weeks ago in Milwaukee, the Police Chief in Bath Township, John Gardner, said. Eric Tyson, who grew up across the street from the Dahmer home, said neighbors had also found frogs and cats impaled or staked to trees, and knew that young Dahmer kept animal skeletons in a backyard shed, near his pet cemetery.

For forensic psychiatrists, such a fascination with death and cruelty to animals is an almost predictable sign in the lives of people accused of being serial killers. As of yesterday, Mr. Dahmer had been charged with killing 12 people in Milwaukee, and the police said he had confessed to the killing of 5 more. Each of the charges against Mr. Dahmer carries a mandatory sentence of life in prison.

"Murderers like this very often start out by killing and torturing animals as kids," said Robert K. Ressler, who developed profiles of serial killers while an agent with the Federal Bureau of Investigation's behavioral sciences unit.

SEVERAL PATTERNS RECOGNIZED

As this and other telling details about Mr. Dahmer have come to light, forensic psychiatrists say they recognize several patterns as gleaned from detailed studies of serial killers.

To be sure, what is known about Mr. Dahmer's history, if verified, offers many signs of a troubled childhood. He told the Milwaukee police that his parents were "constantly at each other's throats" before they divorced. His Army roommate remembered how he desperately wanted to please his father. He told the police that his mother had suffered a nervous breakdown and doted on his younger brother. And, according to what his father told the authorities after he was arrested for molesting a teen-ager in 1986, he had been sexually molested when he was 8 by a boy in the neighborhood.

But the vast majority of those who suffer through such pains of childhood never go on to commit the grisly crimes that Mr. Dahmer says he has committed. Forensic psychiatrists who study the psychology of serial killers seek explanations in deeper emotional currents.

They say Mr. Dahmer's personality, as drawn from the Milwaukee police records and from news reports, shows signs of a particularly dangerous chemistry: an antisocial trait, so that he flouted the law with impunity; a "borderline" personality that makes him vulnerable to explosive rage when he feels he is being abandoned, and a bizarre sexual deviation that culminated in necrophilia.

Of these elements, the most common among serial killers is perversion, forensic experts say. In studies of serial killers, two perversions are most typical: sadism and necrophilia. The sadists find their sexual pleasure in the sufferings of their victims; the sexual thrill stops when the victims die.

'THRILL STARTS WITH DEATH'

But with necrophiliacs, "the thrill starts with the death," said Dr. James Fox, a criminologist at Northeastern University.

In his confession to the Milwaukee police, Mr. Dahmer said that he found sexual pleasure in the body parts he collected from those victims he thought were particularly attractive. He also admitted to having sex with many of his victims after they had died.

"All of these crimes have a sexual basis," said Mr. Ressler, who is now president of Forensic Behavioral Services in Spotsylvania, Va.

"And the more they practice bizarre sexual perversions, the more perverse they get."

Even so, in the making of a serial killer, Mr. Ressler said, "the main thing is not the sexual preferences, but the dynamics of personality."

Perhaps the most striking emotional theme in Mr. Dahmer's life is his dread of being abandoned and alone. While he was in first grade, his mother was ill, and school officials said Mr. Dahmer's teacher noted on his report card that the boy felt "neglected." This sense of neglect seems to hold one key to Mr. Dahmer's personality, forensic psychiatrists say.

Mr. Dahmer complained to the police after his arrest in Milwaukee that as a high school senior his parents left him alone in the house when they were divorced. His father had moved out, and his mother, in defiance of a court order, surreptitiously moved with his younger brother to Wisconsin.

It was at this time that he began having fantasies of killing people. Mr. Dahmer told the police that these fantasies overcame his feelings of frustration and emptiness.

Psychoanalysts say perversions typically originate in reaction to painful emotional feelings. "Sexual perversion is a way of mastering earlier emotional trauma through scenarios that add sexual pleasures to the wound," said Dr. Wayne Myers, a Manhattan psychoanalyst. "It gives you solace, making you feel you have some control over the pain."

FEELINGS OF LONELINESS

It was also when his parents left him alone in the family home, Mr. Dahmer told the police, that he started to feel lonely, began hating to sleep alone at night and felt a strong desire that people not leave him.

"That intense fear of abandonment and intolerance of being alone" is found in people with a 'borderline personality disorder,' " said Dr. Park Dietz, a forensic psychiatrist in Newport Beach, Calif., who is a consultant to the F.B.I. Academy's behavioral science unit.

A hallmark of a borderline personality, in addition to a sense of emptiness and difficulty tolerating being alone, is a frantic effort to avoid abandonment, the psychiatric diagnostic manual says.

"People who fear abandonment can become outraged when someone is about to leave who they want to stay," Dr. Dietz said.

THE FIRST MURDER

That was, apparently, the circumstance of Mr. Dahmer's first murder in mid-1978. Mr. Dahmer told the Milwaukee police that he was living alone in the family home and invited a hitchhiker over for a beer. But when the hitchhiker wanted to leave, Mr. Dahmer said, he became upset, struck him with a barbell and then strangled him.

That same anger at being left was at play in all the other murders, Mr. Dahmer told the police. He would entice men to his apartment by offering them money to pose in the nude. Sometimes he would have sex with them. But, he told the police, it was because he could not bear seeing them leave that he would kill them.

While he would have preferred that his victims remained with him alive, Mr. Dahmer was quoted in a homicide detective's report as saying, "it was better to have them with him dead than to have them leave." Mr. Dahmer also said the reason the killings escalated after he was dismissed from his job was that he was home alone with nothing to do and felt the corpses would keep him company.

The police report said the same gruesome reasoning led Mr. Dahmer to cannibalism, a perversion that the experts say is extremely rare among serial killers. Eating parts of his victims, the detective's report says, "was his way of keeping them with him even longer and making his victims part of himself."

Mr. Dahmer's personality, forensic experts say, seems to harbor another dangerous trait, psychopathy, or an "antisocial personality disorder," as the official diagnosis calls it. The experts pointed to the reports of his cruelty to animals; to what one former high school classmate, Martha A. Schmidt, described as his drinking openly at school, and to his unpredictable wildness.

Mr. Dahmer was so known for pranks like faking epileptic seizures and sneaking into the yearbook picture of the honor society that, some classmates recall, "Don't do a Dahmer" became a current phrase.

NEED FOR HIGH-RISK SITUATIONS

This need to do high-risk things is almost universal among young criminals. "It signifies a biological fearlessness and need to seek thrills that makes criminal risk-taking a high," Dr. Dietz said.

Psychopaths require extremely high-risk situations to get the excitement they crave. They stay calm under circumstances that would make most anyone else anxious, as seems to have been the case when Mr. Dahmer convinced the Milwaukee police to turn over a naked, bleeding teen-ager who had escaped from his apartment, and then to kill him, despite the encounter with the police.

"Serial killers are cool and calculating, in control," Dr. Fox said. "They decide who and how to kill."

Many serial killers keep souvenirs of their victims as "trophies," Dr. Dietz said.

The trophies are usually identification cards or pieces of clothing. But few, Dr. Dietz said, are driven by their loneliness to keep pieces of their victims' bodies. "An ordinary serial killer would have the sense to try to mask the smell," Dr. Dietz said. "It's awfully careless not to."

Milwaukee Jury Says Dahmer Was Sane

BY DIRK JOHNSON | FEB. 16, 1992

JEFFREY L. DAHMER, the serial killer who claimed that sickness drove him to murder and dismember 15 men and boys, was found to be sane by a jury here today.

After two weeks of testimony, the jury rejected arguments by Mr. Dahmer's defense lawyer, Gerald Boyle, that he could not control himself.

The verdicts, returned late this afternoon in Milwaukee County Circuit Court, mean that Mr. Dahmer will be given 15 consecutive life terms in prison when he is sentenced on Monday.

Mr. Dahmer, who has confessed to all 15 killings in his indictment and to two others as well, had pleaded guilty but insane. Had the jury found him insane, he would have been sentenced to a mental institution from which he could have petitioned for release every six months.

The jurors were instructed to base their ruling on two questions: Did Jeffrey Dahmer suffer from mental illness? And if so, did he have "the capacity to appreciate the wrongfulness" of his conduct or "the ability to conform" to law?

Two of the 12 jurors said that Mr. Dahmer was in fact insane, but to reach a finding of insanity under state law, 10 jurors were required.

As the verdicts were read, Mr. Dahmer leaned back in a swivel chair, motionless. Relatives of some of the victims sat across the aisle from Mr. Dahmer's parents, gasping, sobbing and embracing one another.

'KILLING MACHINE'

In closing arguments on Friday, the defense lawyer called Mr. Dahmer a "steamrolling killing machine" who could not control his compulsion to murder. "His willpower was gone," said Mr. Boyle. "He was so

The jury rejected Jeffrey L. Dahmer's insanity plea, finding him sane and guilty on 15 counts of murder. The gruesome murders of 15 men and boys involved rape, necrophilia and cannibalism.

impaired, as he went along this killing spree, that he could not stop. He was a runaway train on a track of madness, picking up steam all the time, on and on and on."

In his rebuttal, the prosecutor described Mr. Dahmer as a cool, calculating killer who cleverly covered his tracks. "He's fooled a lot of people," said District Attorney E. Michael McCann. "Please, please don't let him fool you."

If Mr. Dahmer had taken the stand, his lawyer said, "the perception of him as a human being" would "displace this concept of him being a monster."

But the defendant chose not to testify. "I don't think he could have handled it," Mr. Boyle said.

The prosecution held photographs of each of the victims, urging the jury to remember their suffering. Relatives of the victims wept in the courtroom, and some were led away.

'HE KNEW WHAT HE WAS DOING'

"He knew what he was doing," said Donald Bradehoft, a 33-year-old hotel porter, whose brother was identified as one of Mr. Dahmer's victims. Pinned to his shirt was a photograph of his 25-year-old brother Joseph, whose body was found in Mr. Dahmer's apartment in July. "Dahmer took our loved ones," Mr. Bradehoft said. "He should pay for it — in prison, not a hospital."

Before the verdict was read, relatives of the victims held hands and prayed quietly. Afterward, they lauded the work of the jury. Theresa Smith, whose brother, Albert, was among the victims, said the verdict "brought back the faith I lost in the justice system." Mr. Dahmer sat impassively during most of the trial, wearing a dark suit and looking a bit whiskered and weary. After the lunch recess on Friday, he walked into the courtroom with a copy of the tabloid newspaper Weekly World News that bore a headline saying he had eaten his cellmate at the jail here. The paper's masthead had been replaced with that of The Milwaukee Journal.

"It's amazing what they come up with," Mr. Dahmer said, as he handed the newspaper to Carol Boyle, a sister-in-law of the defense lawyer.

The testimony included discussion of cannibalism, mutilation and sex with corpses. It was revealed that Mr. Dahmer had used a condom while having sex with some of the bodies. The prosecutor cited his desire to avoid sexually transmitted disease as evidence of his sanity.

Some television and radio stations carried the testimony uncensored. But the trial, with its strong doses of absurd and disgusting elements, put the local news media in an awkward position.

"We had a tightrope to walk," said Steve Hannah, the managing editor of The Milwaukee Journal. "On the one hand, we didn't want to assault our readers with gratuitous details. On the other hand, we wanted our readers to appreciate the thrust of the defendant's case that Jeffrey Dahmer is crazy — that what he did was so bizarre, so heinous, that he must be nuts."

Mr. Dahmer's ability to elude police capture, even after officers watched a dazed, naked and bleeding 14-year-old boy run from Mr. Dahmer's apartment, has enraged many gay activists and members of minorities in Milwaukee. They said the police conduct illustrated a lack of concern for the safety of homosexuals. The boy later died, and the officers were dismissed from the force.

In response, Mayor John O. Norquist named a commission to investigate police conduct. The panel said it found instances in which the police had often ignored complaints by homosexuals and minorities.

"Many witnesses perceive that they or their group are singled out routinely for mistreatment and selective enforcement," said the Rev. Albert J. DiUlio, president of Marquette University, who headed the investigation. "That these perceptions bear considerable truth and reality seems beyond question."

Loving Jeffrey Dahmer

BY FRANK RICH | MARCH 17, 1994

EVEN IN A COUNTRY where everything from parricide to political scandal is instantly transformed into a multimedia freak show, the art exhibition that just closed at the Tatou gallery in Beverly Hills might turn heads. There, at prices up to $20,000, connoisseurs purchased paintings by John Wayne Gacy, the condemned serial killer who murdered 33 boys and young men in a Chicago suburb in the 1970's.

"I guess he killed people better than he painted," one patron told The Los Angeles Times. But that doesn't mean there isn't a market for the killer's self-portraits, or that some enterprising scholar won't offer learned views on the parallels between the Gacy oeuvre and, say, the early Hitler watercolors.

This is a boom time for serial killers; they're a growth industry both as a criminal class and as an American cultural preoccupation. As Joyce Carol Oates writes in her survey of serial-killer lit in The New York Review of Books, there have been more serial murders reported since 1970 "than in all previous American history combined." There has also been a run on serial-killer entertainment and merchandise since "Silence of the Lambs" earned its Oscar — from books to documentary films ("Aileen Wuornos: The Selling of a Serial Killer") to artifacts (a proposed auction of Jeffrey Dahmer memorabilia to benefit his victims' families).

Two new names have just joined the pantheon: Henry Louis Wallace, 28, apprehended in Charlotte, N.C., for the murder of 10 women, and Ricardo Silvio Caputo, 44, admitting to four victims at his arraignment in New York. Last week also brought network news-magazine rating triumphs for appearances by Charles Manson and Mr. Dahmer. Mr. Caputo graces ABC's "Prime Time Live" tonight.

What fascinates us about these psychopaths? Ms. Oates's answer is no doubt right: "our uneasy sense that such persons are forms of

Lionel Dahmer, research chemist, author and father of confessed serial killer Jeffrey Dahmer, standing outside of Columbia Correctional Institute, where his son is imprisoned.

ourselves, derailed and gone terribly wrong." Yet it's just as easy to keep a safe distance and see nothing of ourselves in a Ted Bundy or Son of Sam.

Which is why I was shocked when that distance was abruptly narrowed by Lionel Dahmer's just-published "A Father's Story." This blood-free, angst-filled memoir has no prurient passages but it ended my immunity to the national case of the serial-killer creeps.

In measured voice, Mr. Dahmer, a 57-year-old research chemist and the son of teachers, tries to figure out what made his son practice necrophilia and cannibalism on some 17 victims. His task isn't easy because Jeffrey Dahmer does not fit the classic serial-killer pattern. He wasn't an abused child. He grew up not in a foster home but an actual home where he was loved, hugged and indulged despite his parents' divorce and his own alcoholism. Young Jeffrey didn't explode in anger or ramble in conversation. He passed through the S.A.T.'s, state U. and the Army.

"A Father's Story" is illustrated with black-and-white Brownie snapshots of a smiling, tow-headed boy. So what went wrong? Lionel Dahmer is finally reduced to blaming his son's monstrousness on his own unexceptional history. Mr. Dahmer judges himself a poor father because he prattled impersonally about the weather in letters to his son. He also speculates that his own youthful shyness, fascination with bombs and fears of abandonment added up to a monstrous genetic inheritance.

If these were credible theories, this country would have more serial killers than lawyers. Jeffrey Dahmer remains a phantom, defying logic. But if we can't identify with the son, might we not with his caring, intelligent father? Lionel Dahmer so blindly believed in his child that when the police called he at first thought Jeffrey was a murder victim, not a murderer.

Surely none of us would make that mistake. But how certain can we be? Mr. Dahmer's story is terrifying precisely because his blindness to his son's insanity was inseparable from his love for him.

His book's final snapshot, worthy of Diane Arbus, was taken in prison last year. A father-son portrait, it's scarier than any shot in "Silence of the Lambs." The two Dahmers, one a serial killer and one not, stand arm-in-arm, looking just like twins.

I have a picture in my scrapbook that looks something like that. Do you?

Jeffrey Dahmer, Multiple Killer, Is Bludgeoned to Death in Prison

BY DON TERRY | **NOV. 29, 1994**

JEFFREY L. DAHMER, whose gruesome exploits of murder, necrophilia and dismemberment shocked the world in 1991, was attacked and killed today in a Wisconsin prison, where he was serving 15 consecutive life terms.

Mr. Dahmer was 34, older than any of his victims, who ranged in age from 14 to 33. He died of massive head injuries, suffered sometime between 7:50 and 8:10 A.M., when he was found in a pool of blood in a toilet area next to the prison's gym, said Michael Sullivan, secretary of the Wisconsin Department of Corrections. He was pronounced dead shortly after 9 A.M.

A bloodied broomstick was found nearby, and a fellow inmate who is serving life sentence for murder, Christopher J. Scaver, 25, of Milwaukee, is the prime suspect, the authorities said.

E. Michael McCann, the Milwaukee County District Attorney, who sent Mr. Dahmer to prison in 1992, said, "This is the last sad chapter in a very sad life."

"Tragically," Mr. McCann said, "his parents will have to experience the same loss the families of his victims have experienced."

A third inmate, Jesse Anderson, himself a notorious figure in the history of Milwaukee crime and race, was critically injured in the attack.

Mr. Sullivan would not comment on a possible motive for the beatings nor would he say if it was Mr. Dahmer or Mr. Anderson who was the main target of the violence. Mr. Scarver, who is black, was convicted in 1992 of murdering Steve Lohman, who was shot in the head at the Milwaukee office of the Wisconsin Conservation Corps, where he worked, officials said. Mr. Scarver is not eligible for parole until 2042.

But both Mr. Dahmer, whose victims were mostly black, Hispanic and Asian men and boys, and Mr. Anderson, a white man who killed his wife and blamed it on two black men, had badly shaken Milwaukee's racial peace.

Mr. McCann said today, "I hope there will be no economic returns or celebration as a folk hero for the man that killed Jeffrey Dahmer."

"God forbid," he said, "but I would not be surprised if it happened."

Mr. Dahmer and the two other inmates had been assigned to clean the toilets and the showers near the gym and had arrived there under guard at 7:50 A.M.

Then the inmates were apparently left unattended for up to 20 minutes.

"They followed procedures," Mr. Sullivan said of the guards. "There was no irregular gap in supervision."

The three inmates, all convicted murderers, had been on the routine work detail together for about three weeks without incident — until today. At 8:10 A.M., a guard returned to find Mr. Dahmer bleeding on the floor. The guard sounded the alarm and then found Mr. Anderson several rooms away in the shower area.

When Mr. Dahmer arrived at the prison, the Columbia Correctional Institute in Portage, about 40 miles north of Madison, his safety was a major concern.

The blond former chocolate-factory worker was the most prolific killer in the state's history, so, the authorities feared, killing him might earn a convict an honored place in the prison world, especially for someone with a long sentence and with little to lose.

Mr. Dahmer's first year in prison had been spent in protective isolation, away from the general inmate population. But in the last year, Mr. Dahmer and the prison authorities had deemed it safe enough for him to be integrated into the general population of 622 inmates.

Last July, however, an inmate tried to slash Mr. Dahmer's throat with a plastic homemade knife during a chapel service. But Mr. Dahmer was not injured and both he and his keepers determined that the attack was an isolated incident.

"He never told me he was afraid," said Stephen Eisenberg, a lawyer representing Mr. Dahmer in several civil suits filed by the families of his victims. "This shouldn't have happened. Wisconsin does not have a death penalty."

Mr. Dahmer confessed to 17 killings, 16 in Wisconsin and one, his first, he said, in his hometown of Bath Township, Ohio, a well-to-do suburb of Akron. He pleaded guilty and was convicted of 15 killings in Wisconsin. Prosecutors said there was not enough evidence to charge Mr. Dahmer with the 16th slaying.

Mr. Dahmer also pleaded guilty to the Ohio slaying of a young hitchhiker, Steven Hicks, in his parent's home in 1978.

Mr. Dahmer met most of his victims at bus stops, bars, malls and adult bookstores in Chicago and Milwaukee. He then lured them to his apartment in a hard-pressed section of Milwaukee with promises of beer or money in exchange for posing for nude photographs.

Then he would drug their drinks, strangle and stab them while they were unconscious. He ate part of the arm of at least one man and stored the remains, including the hearts, of several others in his refrigerator.

Mr. Dahmer told investigators he killed to ward off loneliness. "I didn't want them to leave," he said.

Mr. Dahmer was almost caught in May 1991 when a 14-year-old Laotian boy, Konerak Sinthasomphone, stumbled into the street bleeding when Mr. Dahmer left the apartment for a six-pack of beer.

Two Milwaukee police officers ignored the pleas of a woman who said the boy was in trouble, and allowed Mr. Dahmer to take him back into his apartment, apparently believing Mr. Dahmer's story that he and the boy were lovers after a spat.

Mr. Dahmer later told investigators that shortly after he got the boy back into his apartment, he killed him. After the Dahmer case broke, the two officers who found the boy bleeding were dismissed, but they won reinstatement last April after a lengthy court battle. One has since left the department.

Mr. Dahmer was finally arrested after another intended victim broke free and ran into the street with a handcuff dangling from his wrist.

While Mr. Dahmer is now dead, the legal battle over his estate remains alive. Several families of his victims sued him and were awarded millions of dollars. Ever since, they have been trying to gain control of the contents of his Milwaukee apartment, where he killed most of his victims.

The families want to auction off some 312 items, including a 55-gallon vat he used to decompose the bodies; the refrigerator where he stored hearts; a saw, a hammer and his toothbrush. Tom Jacobson, the lawyer for the families, said the auction could bring more than $100,000.

Rita Isbell, the sister of one of Mr. Dahmer's last victims, Errol Lindsey, 19, said she always knew that this day would come sooner or later.

For the past two years, she said, she has been getting telephone calls from men identifying themselves as prison inmates, offering condolences and promises that Mr. Dahmer would be "taken care of." The last call came about six months ago.

"You don't know me," Ms. Isbell quoted the caller as saying. "I'm up here with Jeffrey Dahmer. Don't worry. We'll take care of it.' "

Ms. Isbell said she did not know whether the calls were real or pranks. "I wouldn't say I wanted it to happen like this," she said. "But Jeffrey tore my family up."

CHAPTER 6

B.T.K.:
Dennis L. Rader

He couldn't take it anymore. After disappearing for nearly 25 years, the serial killer known as B.T.K. (for bind, torture and kill) sent a new letter to The Wichita Eagle taunting the Wichita, Kan., police to find him. And they did. In 2005, Dennis Lynn Rader was arrested for killing 10 people between 1974 and 1991. Ranging in age from 9 to 62, Rader's victims were each tied up and slowly strangled to death. The killer was caught when police linked metadata on a computer disk of writings he had sent to a local news station to other clues they had collected. Rader is serving 10 consecutive life terms.

Letter From Killer

BY JO NAPOLITANO | MARCH 26, 2004

KANSAS — The police say they believe that a letter recently sent to a local newspaper was written by a serial killer who has eluded the authorities since the 1970's, when seven deaths were attributed to him. The letter, sent to The Wichita Eagle last week, contained a copy of a slain woman's driver's license, which was stolen when she was killed, and grainy images of her body. The woman, Vicki Wegerle, was found dead on Sept. 16, 1986. The police said the killer, known as B.T.K. for his chosen method of murder — bind, torture and kill — probably lived in the Wichita area.

As Serial Killer Reaches Out, Fear Grips Wichita

BY MONICA DAVEY | APRIL 2, 2004

GUNSHOTS, ONE AFTER the next, echoed from a nearby room as Bill Vinduska, the owner of Bullseye, a gun store and indoor shooting range, explained why revolvers, gun training courses, security systems and Mace are suddenly selling so well in an otherwise friendly city like this. Most people here had long ago stopped thinking about Wichita's serial killer of the 1970's, a man who called himself the B.T.K. Strangler for the binding, torturing, killing method he used in at least seven instances back then. The panic of those days — of checking closets before going to bed, of listening for dial tones to be sure phone lines had not been slashed — had faded away. But then a letter turned up, postmarked Wichita, March 17, and the police say they feel sure its author is B.T.K.

So Mr. Vinduska's sales have doubled, and Wichita residents like Danielle Robinson, who said she had never before held a gun, were considering buying weapons. Ms. Robinson said she and her husband were taking other precautions, too, measures eerily reminiscent of routines families adopted here three decades ago when the killer first shocked this city: the dogs stay outside more, lights are left on at night and the Robinsons, poised to dial 911, make a full search of the house each time they come home.

"Who would think you would have to worry in Kansas?" said Ms. Robinson, who moved here from Indiana seven years ago. "But then again, how can you not?"

The killer's first letter — the first of many communications — arrived in the fall of 1974. An editorial writer at a local newspaper, The Wichita Eagle, got a phone call directing him to a letter tucked inside a book at the Wichita Public Library. The writer of the long, detailed letter, packed with misspellings, took responsibility for the unsolved strangling deaths of a family of four, the Oteros, earlier that year. The letter described parts of the crime scene and even made chilling note of Joseph Otero's wristwatch, according to The Eagle. "I needed one so I took it. Runs good," the letter said.

The killing of the Oteros had already shocked Wichita because violent crime was rare. But the notion that the killer was writing everything down, standing in plain view at the library, playing a game with the police left Wichita unnerved.

"That was about when Wichita started to grow up," Mike McKenna, a former police official who tracked the B.T.K. Strangler for years, said the other day.

Over the next five years, the killer struck at least three more times, the police say, with his unique and grotesque methods: watching his victims, slipping into their homes, cutting their phone lines, tying them up with distinctive knots and killing them slowly.

After one death, he sent a poem about his victim, Shirley Vian, to The Eagle. Another time, he called police dispatch from a pay phone in central Wichita and calmly reported on the "homicide" of Nancy Fox and the address where the police would find her body. Another time, he mailed a letter to a woman he had not attacked, just to let her know that he had been in her house, waiting for her, but gave up when she did not return home. That woman, the police say, moved away soon after.

The Wichita police poured years of attention and money into cracking the biggest case to come along. There were different permutations of leads, of patterns, of profiles, of teams of police and outside law enforcement. The best known of the police task forces got the nickname Ghostbusters. And members might as well have been chasing a ghost.

"I would say personally that that's the most frustrating case I've ever encountered," said Richard LaMunyon, the former police chief, who led the force during the peak of the fury.

The truth, Mr. LaMunyon said, was that though the police had chased leads and conducted many stakeouts, they never really got as far as having a firm suspect. Then the leads went cold, and B.T.K. seemed to stop.

In Wichita, people speculated about what had happened to the killer: he might have been sent to prison somewhere, committed to a mental institution or moved. When The Eagle published an article on the 30th anniversary of the first B.T.K. killings this year, plenty of people — some young, some newcomers — had never heard of the killer.

That changed last month, after an envelope arrived in the mailroom of the newspaper. It made its way up to the third-floor newsroom, though it could easily have been forgotten in the piles of reader mail.

"It might well have been tossed," Rick Thames, the paper's editor, said this week. "At first glance, it could have been a prank."

Inside were puzzling images: a photocopy of a woman's driver's license and three fuzzy photocopied photographs of a woman's body lying in front of a television.

A woman matching the name on the license — Vicki Wegerle — had been strangled in September 1986, her killing never solved. Her driver's license had been stolen during the killing. Police technicians took no crime scene photos of Ms. Wegerle because her body had been rushed away by paramedics.

Over the years, the police say, all of B.T.K.'s letters bore a certain distinguishing mark, though the police and others who have seen the letters refused to reveal what it was.

"He has a special way of signing his letters," Mr. McKenna, the former police official, said. "And it's known only to him and to us."

The latest letter bore the sign, too.

Days after the letter arrived, the police announced that B.T.K. was believed to be responsible for the 1986 killing — and also that he was, apparently, back.

That has sent this city of about 350,000, a place where police investigated 21 homicides in 2003 and cleared all of them, back to the 1970's, in a way.

"Now everyone thinks everyone is B.T.K.," Mr. LaMunyon said.

Internet forums about the killer are full of new speculation: does the number 3 have special meaning to B.T.K. because the addresses of all the victims had a 3? Why is he back now? What are the best ways to watch out for him?

The passing of so much time may actually help the police. Technology has advanced. DNA tests not available 30 years ago are being run on old evidence.

Robert Beattie, who is from here, has been writing a book about the case. He said that he had always viewed the work as a history book, but that he had now come to wonder if the ending could turn out to be more dramatic.

Arrest Is Made in
Series of Killings in Kansas

BY MONICA DAVEY | FEB. 27, 2005

WICHITA, KAN., FEB. 26 — People here had often wondered and worried about whether B.T.K., the elusive serial killer who taunted this city on and off for more than three decades, might be living right here, just beside them, all along.

On Saturday, as the authorities announced an arrest in one of the most notorious, puzzling string of crimes in recent history, they confirmed exactly what people in the Wichita area had feared: The man the police had arrested was a longtime neighbor, a leader at one of their churches, a father with a wife and two children, who had once, neighbors said, led a scouting troop for boys.

He was the suburban municipal employee who checked in to see that their dog was on a leash, their garbage can was tucked away, their grass was trimmed just so.

Inside a City Hall chamber packed with the families of victims, scores of police officers, some retired and gray now, and a long line of political leaders from the state, the police announced that they had arrested Dennis L. Rader, 59, of suburban Park City, as the suspect in the case of B.T.K., the name the killer long ago selected for himself for his preferred method: bind, torture, kill.

"The bottom line: B.T.K. is arrested," Chief Norman Williams of the Wichita police said, setting off one of what would become multiple rounds of applause during the announcement that some officials in the room said they had waited their entire careers to hear.

The police said they pulled over Mr. Rader in his vehicle about a block from his home, 10 minutes north of downtown Wichita, just after noon on Friday. He was taken into custody without fuss, the police said, and was being held at an "undisclosed location" on Saturday. He is suspected, said Lt. Ken Landwehr, who worked the B.T.K. mystery for years, in 10 killings — two more than had been publicly attributed to B.T.K. before Saturday.

Mr. Rader has not been charged, but officials said the district attorney's office here would be asked to consider filing charges next week. Neither Mr. Rader nor members of his extended family, many of whom live here, too, could be reached for comment on the case.

The news of an arrest came after a frightened city's 31-year search that included DNA tests on thousands of residents, millions of dollars and work hours expended by police investigators, and a peculiar and public cat-and-mouse game between a killer and an otherwise fairly quiet Kansas community of about 350,000.

For years, B.T.K. sent chilling, taunting letters to anyone, it seemed, who might listen — the police, the local newspaper, television stations — often leaving what appeared to be tantalizing clues about his crimes.

"We knew that our officers were doing their job and that one day this nightmare would end," Mayor Carlos Mayans of Wichita said.

For the families of the dead, the news marked an end of sorts, but also a difficult reminder of their unalterable losses and of how long they had waited. Ruth Fox, the stepmother of Nancy Fox, who was bound and strangled with a nylon stocking in 1977, said she had been stricken by Mr. Rader's image. "When I saw his picture this morning," she said, pausing for a long moment, "I just wanted to choke him."

"There's a sense of closure," she added, "to a degree."

Around Wichita, residents watched the developments with excitement and relief, exchanging detailed gossip about clues in B.T.K. chat rooms on the Internet and calling in to AM-radio talk shows with memories of going to school with Mr. Rader and working with him. Workers at the Wichita airport stood silently around television sets as the news conference played live.

"I think probably starting tonight, there will be some people who sleep soundly for the first time in 30 years," said Robert Beattie of Wichita, who is finishing a book on the case. "I may be one of those people."

Between 1974 and 1979, B.T.K. was suspected in seven killings — the first of his apparently random victims were a 38-year-old retired Air Force mechanic, his wife and two of their children, who were slain in their home — as he taunted police officials and the local news media with letters that provided graphic details of the slayings, chilling poems and even, at one point, a phone call.

Each of B.T.K.'s killings fit a pattern. The killer was diligent, efficient, audacious. He cut telephone lines. He slipped into homes unnoticed. He left his victims bound and killed them slowly.

Then, suddenly, nearly 25 years ago, the killer dropped out of sight. Some people speculated that he had moved away, gone to jail, died.

But just as abruptly, last March, 30 years after the killing had begun, he resurfaced. This time, he wrote a letter to The Wichita Eagle claiming responsibility for an eighth killing, in 1986. That year, Vicki Wegerle, 28, was found strangled at her home. Inside B.T.K.'s letter was a copy of Ms. Wegerle's driver's license and three grainy photographs of her body.

From there, an avalanche of clues — a seeming treasure hunt for the police — has spilled forth from B.T.K. in the past 11 months: detailed letters, jewelry, packages, a cereal box, some in recent weeks.

His letters and poems were often rambling and filled with grammatical and spelling errors. But law enforcement officials gleaned enough information to build a profile of the killer, and late last year they released a string of details to the public, hoping it might help identify him.

But some of the clues the authorities say B.T.K. most recently told them about himself — his birth date in 1939, a father who died in World War II — do not fit Mr. Rader.

The authorities said little on Saturday about what had led them to Mr. Rader. The Sedgwick County district attorney, Nola Foulston, said that she and other officials would not give any details on statements that investigators might have taken, evidence gathered or forensic tests until charges were filed.

But Gov. Kathleen Sebelius, attending the winter meeting of the National Governors Association in Washington, told The Associated Press that state highway patrol officials familiar with the case had told her that investigators had definitely linked Mr. Rader to the slayings.

"The way they made the link was some DNA evidence, that they had some DNA connection to the guy who they arrested," Ms. Sebelius said.

And Richard LaMunyon, the former police chief here who led the force during the peak of the B.T.K. search years ago, said he believed that "advances in technology" — both DNA evidence and computer records — had finally helped investigators solve the case.

Looking back, Mr. LaMunyon said he believed that Mr. Rader might have been in a broad field of people investigators considered as possible suspects sometime in the past. At one point, based on similarities between the particular wording of one of B.T.K.'s poems and a poem in a college textbook, the authorities announced that they were considering students who had taken an American folklore class at Wichita State University. Mr. Rader graduated from Wichita State in 1979 with a degree in the administration of justice.

Mr. Rader, who has worked for more than a decade as a municipal compliance officer in Park City, also lived only a few doors down the street from where another murder victim had lived — one that had never been publicly described as a B.T.K. case until Saturday.

In that case, Marine Hedge, 53, was abducted from her home in 1985. Her strangled body was found eight days later along a dirt road. A 10th case, also connected publicly to B.T.K. for the first time on Saturday, also involved a victim who lived not far from the Rader home. That death, in 1991, would be B.T.K.'s most recent killing.

In Park City, Mr. Rader was known for wandering the subdivision roads in his city truck, wearing his official tan city uniform, and stopping in whenever he saw potential violations of the city's rules. Mr. Rader knew every lawn, every house in the community of about 6,000. Sometimes, neighbors said, he would march right into their backyards and snap photographs to show leaky roofs or overflowing trash. He was persnickety about code violations, even pushy, people said, but he certainly never struck them as dangerous or even particularly interesting.

"You always wondered if it was someone you knew, someone in your own backyard, but this is ridiculous," Zach Day, 30, said of B.T.K. "How could this be?"

Mr. Day's mother, Linda, thought back on all the times she said she had talked back to Mr. Rader, arguing with his demands that she move her trash can. "He could have come in anyone's door anytime he liked," she said. "In fact, he did. You wouldn't have thought a thing of it. There was nothing to be scared of. And that's what's so scary."

Mr. Rader's wife, who worked at a nearby convenience store, is popular here. Their two children — now in their late 20's — grew up here.

At Christ Lutheran Church in Wichita, Mr. Rader was president of the church council and a member for about 30 years. On Saturday, members of the congregation were reeling and its leaders met in private.

"Everyone must be glad" about news of an arrest in the B.T.K. case, the pastor's wife, Jan Clark, said sadly, "so that healing can begin for the families of the victims."

She added, "What I want the public to do is pray for this family and for the congregation members who thought they knew this man."

GLEN SHARP contributed reporting from Wichita for this article.

Computer Disk Led to Arrest in Killings, Pastor Says

BY MONICA DAVEY | MARCH 2, 2005

WICHITA, KAN., MARCH 1 — In the end, the B.T.K. serial killer's downfall may have been his own love of sending letters, poems and packages out to the world.

Michael G. Clark, the pastor of Dennis L. Rader, the man now charged with 10 counts of murder in the strangulations that terrorized a city, said Tuesday that one item in the killer's most recent mailing to a local television station helped finally crack the case: an ordinary computer disk.

The police here have refused to say what led them to arrest Mr. Rader, a city codes enforcer and a church leader, 31 years after the first killings in Wichita, but they have acknowledged that the B.T.K. serial killer's peculiar and persistent communications with the public, particularly in recent months, worked to their advantage in the investigation.

Mr. Clark said that the police told him they used information on the computer disk in B.T.K.'s final mailing on Feb. 16 to trace it back to a computer at Christ Lutheran Church, where Mr. Clark is the pastor. Mr. Rader, the president of the church council, had used the church's computer a few weeks earlier, Mr. Clark said, to print the agenda for a council meeting he was to preside over.

"I remember showing him how to use the computer, how to use the printer, because his wasn't working at home," said Mr. Clark, whose church office was searched by the police last week, a day before the police announced the arrest. "What the investigators found, from what I understand, running that disk through scanning and processing, was that that disk had to have been in our computer."

So, it seems, the killer who suggested that he be called B.T.K. (for bind, torture, kill) in his rambling, eerie mailings in the 1970's may have been ensnared by technology.

Mr. Rader, 59, appeared before a judge on Tuesday for the first time, listening as 10 charges of first-degree murder were read aloud. Mr. Rader, who appeared through a videoconference from the county jail, stood somberly, hands crossed before him, lips pursed. Asked whether he understood the charges he faced, Mr. Rader answered in a loud clear voice, "Yes, sir."

Though Mr. Rader could not see them from the jail, about a dozen relatives of victims linked to the case sat in the courtroom. As they filed out, they were ashen faced and silent.

In the hearing, which lasted a few minutes, Mr. Rader was appointed three public defenders, the first formal representation he has had since his arrest on Friday. Sarah E. McKinnon, an assistant public defender, said a short time later that the defense team had not yet met with Mr. Rader but intended to meet with him later on Tuesday. Ms. McKinnon said she expected a delay in a preliminary hearing now set for March 15, where Mr. Rader will have the opportunity to enter a plea.

When the killings began here in 1974, so did B.T.K.'s writings, the police said. He sent them to television stations, left them in libraries and mailed them to the local newspaper. Back then, they were often graphic descriptions of his grisly work, drawings or angry diatribes.

After a poem he had sent to The Wichita Eagle-Beacon was accidentally misplaced in the classified advertising department, he sent an angry letter to a television station saying, "How many do I have to kill before I get my name in the paper or some national attention?"

Then, just as suddenly as the letters had begun, they stopped in 1979.

The silence lasted 25 years — until March, when more packages and letters began arriving at a furious pace. They were left in parks and sent to news outlets, 11 mailings in all. They included a word puzzle, chapter headings for a proposed telling of the B.T.K. tale, a Post Toasties cereal box and a postcard. They were strangely more polite than the earlier letters, one even inquiring about the well-being of television reporters who had, at some point, mentioned on the air having had the flu.

The last one arrived on Feb. 16 at KSAS-TV. At the request of the police, reporters at KWCH-TV, Channel 12, which produces the newscasts for KSAS, did not report on the air all that was in the manila envelope.

But they shared the contents this week: an ornate necklace, perhaps a victim's; a copy of the inside cover of "Rules of Prey," a book about a serial killer by John Sandford; and a lilac-colored computer disk.

"We have been told that the package was instrumental in leading to the arrest," Roger Cornish, an anchor at KWCH, said in an interview on Tuesday.

Mr. Clark, the pastor, said he did not fully understand the technology the police described using in tracing a disk to a single computer.

But Drake Pruitt of Bocada Inc. of Bellevue, Wash., a software company that deals with questions about data recovery, said there were at least two ways a disk might reveal where it had been. Old files that seem to be erased might actually still be accessible on the disk, or the disk might preserve an Internet protocol address, particular to an individual computer that is attached to the Internet. "There frankly could be many forms of digital signature on a disk," Mr. Pruitt said.

Mr. Clark, who has met with Mr. Rader's family since the arrest, said that news reports that Mr. Rader's daughter, who is in her 20's and lives in Michigan, had "turned her father in" to the police were inaccurate. He said the thought of that was deeply upsetting to an already stricken family.

What was true, Mr. Clark said, was that the authorities in Michigan approached Mr. Rader's daughter and sought a DNA sample from her as a way of comparing DNA left at some of the killings with a strain in Mr. Rader's family.

"She gave the DNA for the purpose of clearing her dad," said Mr. Clark, who said he was visiting with Mr. Rader's wife, Paula, when their daughter called, distraught. "She was caught in the middle of all this chaos."

The Wichita police and F.B.I. agents in Michigan and Kansas refused to comment on any DNA testing. Charles Nebus, the director of public safety in Farmington, Mich., the town of 11,000 where Mr. Rader's daughter lives, said he received a call from F.B.I. agents on Friday, alerting him that they were in his region conducting an interview and asking "a procedural question" about collecting DNA.

Early Tuesday, Mr. Clark said he had yet to visit Mr. Rader, a 30-year member of the church, in jail, but hoped to soon. On Sunday night, he said, he received a phone message from Mr. Rader, asking in a quiet, calm voice to see his pastor.

GRETCHEN RUETHLING contributed reporting from Chicago for this article.

Suspect in 10 Kansas Murders Lived an Intensely Ordinary Life

BY MONICA DAVEY | MARCH 6, 2005

PARK CITY, KAN., MARCH 5 — In his crisp beige uniform, cap and badge, Dennis L. Rader took his job upholding the most mundane city laws with unusual earnestness.

He was often seen in his white truck, the words "Compliance Officer, Park City" painted on the side, puttering along at 10 miles an hour, searching for overgrown lawns, overflowing trash cans or dogs wandering past their fences.

"He looked for absolutely everything, and he must have enforced every rule there ever was — just because he could, I guess," said Barbara Walters, 69, a retired auditor for the Internal Revenue Service, who challenged a $25 ticket that Mr. Rader issued in 1998, saying her dog, Shadow, was running loose.

Ms. Walters's lawyer said Mr. Rader arrived for court more prepared than some lawyers are for murder trials, bearing a lengthy file on Shadow, a videotape of the dog and a complicated system of notebook tabs linking the accusations to his evidence. Mr. Rader, and his pile of paper, won.

But the police say the man who was a stickler for the slightest pet infraction in this modest suburb of Wichita had also slain 10 people by then, as the killer known as B.T.K.

Investigators say that Mr. Rader, who will turn 60 on Wednesday, almost certainly in the solitary jail cell where he has been held since he was charged last week with 10 counts of murder, is one of the nation's most notorious and elusive serial killers, the strangler who toyed with Wichita for three decades in letters and poems and packages and who long ago insisted that the public call him B.T.K., for his preferred method: bind, torture, kill. Lawyers for Mr. Rader, who has yet to enter a plea in the case, did not return calls.

The exterior of Christ Lutheran Church in Park City, Kan., where Dennis L. Rader attended Sunday services each week. Rader was arrested on suspicion of first-degree murder in connection with the 10 deaths now tied to the serial killer known as B.T.K.

Most stunning for the Wichita area, where Mr. Rader has spent his life, is not just that he was viewed as an ordinary fellow, someone who blended in at the Taco Bell, but that he seemed to have stayed meticulously and constantly within the strictest mores of society — more so, at times, than many other residents.

Mr. Rader and his wife of 34 years went to church each Sunday. Sometimes when he left an after-work bar outing to hurry home, his colleagues would privately breathe a sigh of relief; with him gone, they could drink up and tell off-color jokes. As far back as the eighth grade, Mr. Rader was picked for the prestigious school patrol, who carried big red Stop signs and told classmates and drivers when to go and when not to.

"The thing to remember is that we always thought in the end that B.T.K. would be a local, that he would probably even be a functioning member of the community," said Richard LaMunyon, who led the

Wichita Police Department at the height of the investigation years ago. "But I guess we never dreamed he would be functioning quite to this degree — a church leader, a Boy Scout leader, someone quite so known, quite so public."

Many serial killers have led relatively successful lives, with steady jobs and relationships, in contrast with their popular image as loners and drifters. But experts on serial killings say that the portrait of Mr. Rader takes that notion of stability, authority and prominence in the community to a level rarely seen.

In Wichita, where a generation of police officers spent their careers searching for B.T.K. — deconstructing his tangled, grisly writings, studying dozens of psychological profiles and swabbing DNA from the cheeks of 4,000 residents — some older detectives have now come to Mr. LaMunyon wondering whether they should have found Mr. Rader, who was hardly hiding away, decades sooner. After all, his name should have appeared on at least two broad lists of suspects in the 1970's, Mr. LaMunyon said, and Mr. Rader had other tenuous ties to 3 of the 10 victims.

Born on March 9, 1945, Dennis Lynn Rader was the eldest of four boys who grew up in a working-class neighborhood in Wichita, a city of fewer than 170,000 then. His father, Bill, who died in 1996 after retiring as a plant operator at a utility company's generating station, was strict but never cruel, Mr. Rader's childhood friends recalled.

"Raders are a little bit stubborn, but not mean," said Lee Rader, 73, who was a first cousin of Bill Rader and lives in Springfield, Mo. Like much of the extended family in sturdy towns across the Midwest, Lee Rader said he could not remember a time when Bill Rader's family had done anything that might draw notice, much less cross the law. "There is some divorces, I guess that's the worst thing that's going," he said.

Dennis Rader's young life seemed uncomplicated and happily ordinary to Roger Farthing, who grew up with him. Mr. Rader buried himself in dime-store novels and comic books. He played cops and robbers until dark. And he posed a question to the teacher on the first day of the first grade, a question few here let him forget: What time is lunch?

Years later, Mr. Rader reminisced on that simpler time. In the "Riverview Round-Up," a questionnaire for his grade-school reunion, he listed his favorite memories in big block letters: recess, story times, last days of school, snowball fights broken up by the principal, art class, a nearby candy store, an old merry-go-round and, of course, lunch hour. Asked for any "pearls of wisdom," Mr. Rader wrote: "Do it now. Life is complicated and short so stay young at heart as long as possible: It was so easy in '59."

After high school, Mr. Rader tried several semesters at two colleges but soon joined the Air Force, learning to repair wire and antenna systems, and leaving Wichita for four years, the longest he would ever be away. He returned in 1970 and settled down with Paula Dietz, who had grown up here, too, gone to the same high school, and lived just around the corner from the squat house in Park City where they would soon have a boy, Brian, and a girl, Kerri.

While attending a community college, Mr. Rader worked for a year on an assembly line at the Coleman Company, making heating and cooling units. From 1973 to 1979, he took classes at Wichita State University, earning a bachelor's degree. His major was criminal justice.

THE KILLINGS BEGIN

On Jan. 15, 1974, B.T.K. struck Wichita for the first time, although most residents would not learn those initials, or even that a serial killer was on the loose, for several years.

The scene was ghastly, unlike anything this city had seen before. Four members of the Otero family — Joseph, 38, a retired Air Force officer; Julie, 34, who had worked at the Coleman Company about a month before; and two of their children, Josephine, 11, and Joseph II, 9 — were strangled inside their home in the middle of the day with the cord used in Venetian blinds.

Left behind was a uniquely grisly scene, and one whose details would be echoed in the future killings. The phone line had been cut. The Oteros had been bound, and the police noted that the knots were particularly elaborate. The killer had taken at least one souvenir of the day: a watch.

None of the Oteros had been sexually assaulted, though Josephine's body was found partly clothed, hanging from a sewer pipe in the basement. Not far from the girl, there in the basement, semen was found, as it would be in subsequent killings. Investigators quickly believed they were searching for a sexual deviant, someone who took pleasure in tying people up, watching them gasp for air and die slowly. Some of the victims' faces were left bloated, investigators said, suggesting that the killer would strangle them, let them breathe, then strangle them some more.

The Otero case would be the first and last known time that B.T.K. would kill a man or a child: the rest of the victims were all women, seemingly picked at random, and in ages ranging from 21 to 62 years old. Nine months later, after the police announced a possible confession in the Otero case, the killer's first letter appeared. It took credit for the Otero deaths, mentioned details that the police said only the killer would have known, and expressed frustration that someone else might be trying to assume credit for the deaths. The letter was riddled with typographical and spelling errors.

"I can't stop it so the monster goes on, and hurt me as well as society," the letter said. He noted that he would be "waiting in the dark, waiting, waiting," and closed the letter with a postscript: "The code words for me will be Bind them, toture them, kill them, B.T.K., you see he at it again. They will be on the next victim."

But by then the killer had already struck again. Kathryn Bright, who also worked at Coleman, was stabbed to death inside her house in April. Her phone lines were snipped, and she was bound with a knotted cord.

IN THE SECURITY BUSINESS

Soon after Mr. Rader started a job at ADT, the security company, at the end of 1974, he was widely disliked — particularly by those beneath him after he became supervisor for the alarm installers.

"He was deeply competent, organized, and good at what he did, but he was a taskmaster," said Rick Carr, 68, who sold systems for ADT. "He came in with the attitude: you're here to get the job done, and I'm not here to be someone's pal."

In his gray ADT uniform shirt with "Dennis" above the pocket, Mr. Rader worked for 14 years in what others called "the dungeon," the section of the office with no windows, gray walls and a steel door. But his job also sent him out of the office during the day regularly, to sign off on installations.

At company swimming pool parties at the Carrs' home in Wichita, Martha Carr, Mr. Carr's former wife, said Mr. Rader always arrived cheerily with his wife and children, looked people right in the eye and said all the right things: that the party was lovely, the food was nicely arranged.

Paula Rader, meanwhile, was a fabulous cook and a quiet, sweet woman who seemed to have a loving, happy marriage, Ms. Carr said. "She seemed innocent," Ms. Carr said, "not worldly, you know?"

One regular topic of discussion at ADT, not surprisingly, was B.T.K.

"It was the conversation all over town, but this was a security company, and let's face it — B.T.K. increased our business," said Denise Mattocks, 46, who worked alongside Mr. Rader for years.

Ms. Mattocks, who was single at the time, was particularly fearful of B.T.K., she said, and told Mr. Rader so regularly. Like so many in Wichita as the panic grew, she spoke of checking her telephone for a dial tone every time she got home. Mr. Rader, she recalled, said little in response. If anything, his efforts at conversation leaned more to his life at home: his wife, the tomatoes in his garden, his Boy Scout outings.

Mr. Rader became a Scout leader when his son, Brian, was about 8 and could join Pack 491. Mr. Rader held the boys to strict standards, not letting them slide by, as some fathers did, without perfecting skills for a badge, said George J. Martin, 70, who helped lead the pack. Mr. Rader was particularly capable, Mr. Martin said, when it came to the knots the boys had to learn.

"The sheepshank, the bowline, the half hitch, the monkey fist," he remembered, "Dennis knew them all."

THE LETTERS STOP

By the late 1970's, B.T.K. had killed seven people, the police say, and the eerie, taunting letters kept arriving. One letter was traced to a copier at Wichita State University. And in 1979, after B.T.K. apparently broke into a widow's home and waited — without success — for her to come home, he sent a poem to the woman who never arrived: "Oh, Anna Why Didn't You Appear."

In part, the poem read: "Alone again I trod in pass memory of mirrors, and ponder why for number eight was not." And then the letters suddenly stopped. The police say B.T.K. killed three more women in 1985, 1986 and 1991 — including two cases, one from Park City and another from nearby, that were not linked to B.T.K. publicly until last weekend.

Some people, like Al Thimmesch, a retired Wichita police officer, wonder whether more deaths have yet to be identified as the work of B.T.K. But if the police are right, the serial killings ended on Jan. 19, 1991, with the death of Dolores Davis, whose house is near Park City.

In May 1991, Mr. Rader was hired as a Park City compliance officer, a period one resident of this suburb just north of Wichita calls the start of the "reign of terror" for homeowners here. Mr. Rader's critics here say he seemed to sit in his truck, just waiting for something to go wrong with their houses. He took numerous photos of their homes, they said, in search of something awry. Some people even insist that he sometimes let their dogs out himself, then cited the owners.

Rhonda Reno said she watched one day as Mr. Rader wandered on the lawn of a neighbor who was ill and unable to mow the grass. Walking the grass with a yardstick, she said, he measured for infractions. "I never trusted him," said Jim Reno, her husband. "There were two people I keep an eye on in this block and one was him."

Still, others here liked Mr. Rader, and found his outsized enthusiasm for his inspection work charming.

He helped an elderly resident trap skunks, and helped his neighbor, a single woman, by mowing her lawn and fixing her leaky faucets, the neighbor said. And even he could bend the rules. Another woman, Virginia Jackson, 53, recalled when her boxer got loose and Mr. Rader chased down the dog and, after a struggle, managed to bring it home. Ms. Jackson never got a ticket.

"He was very professional," she said. "He was doing his job."

BREAKING HIS SILENCE

Last January, The Wichita Eagle published an article about B.T.K. to mark the 30th anniversary of the Otero killings and the start of the panic. By then, the case had been forgotten by many. The article suggested that B.T.K. might have moved away or even died.

Two months later, B.T.K. wrote a letter, his first in a quarter century. From there, he embarked on a communication frenzy — 10 letters or packages mailed to newspapers and media outlets, or simply left in parks. He filled these, too, with trinkets, some apparently from the killings: photographs, a word puzzle, a doll with a plastic bag over its head, a necklace, a computer disk and a victim's driver's license.

By last weekend, with help from the disk and DNA evidence, the police took Mr. Rader into custody and announced with great fanfare that B.T.K. had been caught.

Looking back, some people wonder if the Wichita police could have made an arrest sooner. Mr. LaMunyon, the former police chief, tells those who ask that he does not believe an arrest was possible over all those years; the B.T.K.'s newest mailings, many of which contained a mellower, more conciliatory tone than years before, created a whole new room full of evidence for investigators to go on.

Still, he acknowledged that Mr. Rader's name was probably included on two long lists drawn up by the police years ago. The police had gathered the names of Coleman employees at one point because the first two women killed had worked there, as had, it turned out, Mr. Rader. They had also collected the names of white men at Wichita

State in the 1970's because they knew that one of B.T.K.'s letters had been copied on campus and that a poem sent by B.T.K. resembled a song taught in a popular professor's folklore seminar at Wichita State.

There was another link, too. Although the police had not publicly connected the death of Marine Hedge, the eighth victim, to B.T.K. until last weekend, at the time of her death, Ms. Hedge lived six houses down the street from Mr. Rader's home in Park City.

"I think the police made a mistake over the years," said Robert Beattie, a Wichita lawyer who is writing a B.T.K. book. "They were looking for a Charles Manson type."

Charles Liles, a former Wichita police officer, said the police focused too narrowly on convicted sex offenders rather than someone who might live right among them.

The Rev. Michael G. Clark, Mr. Rader's pastor, visited him in jail on Wednesday, a glass wall between the pastor and his church council president. Mr. Rader is "doing as well as can be expected," Mr. Clark said. His own disbelief, though, has not worn off. The more he reflects, Mr. Clark said, the more he remembers only ordinary conversations with Mr. Rader, talks about fishing and his mother's health.

"That's what I've realized," Mr. Clark said. "There is nothing to remember, nothing that would make it all make sense."

Park City, meanwhile, quietly fired Mr. Rader last week, saying only that he had failed to show up for work or to call.

ARIEL HART contributed reporting from Atlanta for this article, **MICHAEL MCELROY** from Wichita and **GRETCHEN RUETHLING** from Chicago.

Kansas Suspect Pleads Guilty in 10 Murders

BY JODI WILGOREN | JUNE 28, 2005

CHICAGO, JUNE 27 — The serial killer who taunted residents of Wichita, Kan., for three decades pleaded guilty on Monday to 10 murders, calmly and politely recounting his crimes in horrific detail in a court hearing as victims' relatives stoically absorbed the sordid story.

Dennis Rader, 60, a former Boy Scout leader and church president who in poems and packages sent to news outlets nicknamed himself B.T.K. — for bind, torture, kill — referred to his victims as "projects" as he answered questions from a judge in a Wichita courtroom, and said strangling them had been part of a sexual fantasy. Repeatedly calling the judge sir, Mr. Rader methodically described trolling neighborhoods in search of prey, plucking names from mailboxes and stalking women to work, but he said he also picked at least one target at random.

"Potential hits, in my world, that's what I called them," he said, occasionally closing his eyes or rubbing his forehead as he spoke in a monotone. "If one didn't work out, I just moved to another one."

He told of placating one woman's crying children with blankets and toys in the bathtub while he cinched a rope around her neck. He said he used a pillow and parka to make a man with a broken rib more comfortable before placing a plastic bag over his head. He recalled masturbating after hanging Josephine Otero, 11, in the basement of her home.

He explained that he carried "hit kits" — a briefcase or bowling bag filled with rope and other supplies — parked his car blocks away and talked his way into homes by saying he was a repairman, a fugitive or a private detective. He offered no motive other than sexual fantasy, and spoke of putting victims "down," as a veterinarian might a dog.

Recounting the 1974 slaying of four members of the Otero family, Mr. Rader said, "I had never strangled anyone before, so I really didn't know how much pressure you had to put on a person or how long it would take."

Three years later, wielding a .357 Magnum as he confronted the woman he called Project Green — Shirley Vian, 24 — in her "night robe," he recalled, "I explained to her that I'd done this before."

Steve Osburn, the public defender, said that his client pleaded guilty because he "basically wanted to take responsibility for his actions" but that lawyers had also determined that an insanity defense was unrealistic. "From a legal standpoint, we had nothing to work with."

Mr. Rader, who worked at a security company and as a compliance officer for a Wichita suburb, faces consecutive life sentences when he returns to court Aug. 17. He admitted to killings from 1974 to 1991, when Kansas did not have the death penalty. The pleas, which were not part of a deal with prosecutors, stunned but satisfied many people connected with the case in Wichita and the surrounding towns in central Kansas, where Mr. Rader lived his double life. Law enforcement officials, politicians, relatives of those involved and ordinary citizens expressed shock at the graphic, detached presentation Mr. Rader gave in court but also relief that the community would be spared the expense and emotion of a lengthy trial.

Jeff Davis, whose mother, Dolores, was Mr. Rader's final victim, likened the killer's emotionless display on Monday to someone "reading out of a phonebook," and denounced him as "a rotting corpse of a wretch of a human hiding under a human veneer."

"He was putting on Serial Murderer 101 for us," Mr. Davis said. "I'm spiteful, I'm vengeful, and I relish the thought that he knows that he'll walk into that prison but he'll be carried out." While the guilty pleas cannot bring his mother back, he added, "I do have the answers I've been praying for for 14 years."

Mr. Rader spoke for more than an hour, under questioning by Judge Greg Waller in the Sedgwick County Courthouse, his tale beamed live on local and national television stations. He wore a bulletproof vest under an ivory sport coat and blue necktie, and asked his lawyers for a glass of water before admitting, as the judge said repeatedly, that he had killed 10 people "maliciously, deliberately, willfully and by premeditation."

The murders of the Otero family were his first. After killing them he took a radio and a watch, he said, but added, "I have no idea why I took them."

In 1977, he said, he sneaked into 25-year-old Nancy Fox's apartment, snipped her phone lines and waited in the kitchen for her to come home. "I confronted her and told her I had sexual problems and I'd have to tie her up and have sex with her," Mr. Rader recalled. "She was a little upset. We talked for a while and she smoked a cigarette and I went through her purse. She finally said, 'Well, let's get this over with so I can call the police.' "

But Mr. Rader did not rape Ms. Fox — indeed, there was no evidence of sexual assault of any of his victims, though semen was sometimes found at the scene. Instead, he lay on top of her, both of them undressed, and masturbated after she was dead.

Eight years later, Mr. Rader hid in the bathroom of Marine Hedge, 53, who lived down the street from him in the tidy town of Park City, Kan. "She knew me casually," he said. "She liked to work in her yard. It was just a neighborly type thing."

Afterward, Mr. Rader said, he took Ms. Hedge's nude body in the trunk of his car to Christ Lutheran Church — where later he was elected president of the council — and took some pictures of her in "bondage positions" with a Polaroid.

Roger Farthing, who went to school with Mr. Rader, said watching the hideous testimony was like seeing a "second person" inhabit his old friend's body. "I was watching Dennis Rader tell someone else's story today," Mr. Farthing said.

Carlos Mayans, the mayor of Wichita, said in a statement that "prayers have been answered," and wished for "a new chapter in our community." The state's attorney general, Phill Kline, said the pleas brought a "three-decade nightmare" to an end, while Gov. Kathleen Sebelius said, "I hope and pray it will provide some measure of solace and closure to the victims' families."

After 17 years of killings accompanied by anonymous letters and phone calls claiming responsibility, B.T.K. was silent from the 1991 killing of Ms. Davis, 62, until early 2004. After The Wichita Eagle published an article marking the 30th anniversary of the Otero killings, postcards and packages containing clues and trophies — victims' driver's licenses, a doll — turned up in local newsrooms, libraries, a park and a police station. Mr. Rader was arrested in February, when a computer disk he sent was traced to his church. Many people believed he wanted to be caught.

On Monday, when Judge Waller asked whether he had a history of psychological problems, Mr. Rader said, "No, your honor." Mr. Rader said he was satisfied with his lawyers and that the court "has been very fair."

"Are you pleading guilty because you are guilty?" the judge asked.

Yes, Mr. Rader replied, adding, "I think a trial would just be a long process to guilty."

BUD NORMAN and GLEN SHARP contributed reporting from Wichita for this article, and GRETCHEN RUETHLING from Chicago.

Shadows at Home: Living Where B.T.K. Killed

BY MICHAEL WILSON | JUNE 29, 2005

WICHITA, KAN., JUNE 28 — There are six of them left, homes of different sizes, different styles, different neighborhoods, but lumped together by the same dark past and known throughout town by the same name.

The B.T.K. houses.

Greg Lietz, 47, who works at a clothing retailer, bought his small ranch-style house on Edgemoor Street in 1999, but said he did not learn the history of the place until about a year later, on Halloween.

"I got decorations and stuff, and nobody came to the door," Mr. Lietz said. "I asked someone. They said somebody had murdered the family at home. Four people."

The serial killer who called himself B.T.K. in letters to reporters — for bind, torture, kill — murdered 10 people in Wichita and remained at large for three decades. On Monday, Dennis Rader, 60, pleaded guilty to all 10 murders in a long and detailed courtroom account of each murder so graphic and chilling that news stations replayed it late that night with a warning to parents.

But for the residents who chose to buy — or, like Mr. Lietz, found that they had already bought, obliviously — one of the houses where there had been a murder, Mr. Rader's confession quite literally hit closer to home. In the same flat monotone and for the first time publicly, he described strangulations, masturbation and even the victim's last words in the very rooms where these people now cook, relax, work and sleep.

Connie Pouyamehr, 52, a cashier at a grocery store, watched the replay Monday on the late news, in her home. There, on April 27, 1985, Mr. Rader broke in — just six doors down from his own family's home on Independence Street — with a bowling bag for what he called his "hit kit," and he waited for Marine Hedge, whom he had been stalking.

"She came in with a male visitor," Mr. Rader recounted in court. He said he hid in the bathroom until the man left, and then attacked Ms. Hedge in her bedroom. "She screamed," he said. "I jumped on the bed and strangled her manually." Her body was found the following week in a roadside ditch.

Ms. Pouyamehr, asked to describe hearing the confession the next day, snapped: "What do you think it was like? I'm horrified by the whole thing, not just what happened in my house."

Ms. Pouyamehr bought the house — a ranch-style home with three bedrooms and cedar siding — six years after the murder, believing that Ms. Hedge had been kidnapped there, but did not know until Monday that she had been killed in the home, too. Like Ms. Hedge, she knew Mr. Rader and his wife, Paula, as neighbors, regularly carrying her garden tomatoes down to their home. Now, the street is a draw for reporters, crime buffs and the curious.

"We've got people who, after church, like to stop and show their kids where B.T.K. lived," she said. "After church."

Ronald Hudson, a 48-year-old construction worker, moved into his half of a white duplex on Pershing Street three months ago, undeterred when the landlord told him that Nancy Fox had been killed there in 1977. "It's a nice area, quiet, and the price is right," Mr. Hudson said. Before he moved in, two previous tenants took off as soon as they heard what had happened, the landlord told him.

Mr. Hudson watched closely on Monday as Mr. Rader described hiding in the kitchen, allowing Ms. Fox a last cigarette before strangling her. He went to look for himself: "I got up and went to the kitchen and said, 'How did he break into this woman's house and wait in the kitchen and her not have heard anything?' "

Next door, William Stofer, 23, who is also a construction worker, said he believed that Ms. Fox's spirit haunted the two adjoining apartments, as he hears unexplained noises in the kitchen almost every night. Once, Mr. Stofer said, he and his girlfriend found their indoor grill plugged in and warming when neither had touched it. They called the police, who found nothing. "I heard she got strangled in the kitchen," he said. "It kind of spooks me out."

Diane Boyle, 54, a retired nurse, said she was furious when she learned, months after she bought a vinyl-sided bungalow built in the 1940's on South Hydraulic Street in the winter of 2002, that B.T.K. had killed Shirley Vian Relford there in 1977.

Ms. Boyle said she told a neighbor one day, "I know the B.T.K. killer was around here," thinking it was up or down the street. "The Realtor never told me," she said. "I asked my neighbor, and she said, 'Well, Diane, it's your house.' "

In the real estate business, such a house is known as a "stigmatized property," but there is no rule in Kansas that requires real estate agents to disclose anything beyond material information, like a leaking roof or unsound walls, said Frank Stucky, president of the Wichita Area Association of Realtors.

"I don't know of any hard and fast rule other than common sense," Mr. Stucky said. "Certainly in a B.T.K thing, in my mind that would fall under the rule of being something that someone would want to know about."

Ms. Boyle said that had she known, she probably would have bought the house anyway, but that she "wouldn't have paid as much." She said the dead woman's son — who, just a young boy in 1977, had unknowingly let Mr. Rader into the home — had visited twice when he was in town for Mr. Rader's court appearances.

All the residents interviewed said that a British psychic, Dennis McKenzie, visited their homes last year, before Mr. Rader's arrest, to try to help solve the case by extracting images from the walls. Most have come to accept inquisitive strangers. One B.T.K. house, where Kathryn Bright was stabbed on East 13th Street, was torn down, leaving six.

On Independence Street, Ms. Pouyamehr has long been tired of the upkeep on her aging home and wants to move. "I just want a nice, new house, you know?" she said. "I think every woman wants a nice, new house once in their life."

She wants to get away from Independence, too. "It used to be a nice, quiet neighborhood," she said.

Up the street, a sign posted on Mr. Rader's lawn announced that the killer's three-bedroom home would be sold at auction on July 11. His family has moved out, and pictures of the vacant interior are posted on the real estate agent's Web site. Like any other house.

10 Life Terms for B.T.K. Strangler as Anguished Families Condemn Him in Court

BY JODI WILGOREN | AUG. 19, 2005

WICHITA, KAN., AUG. 18 — A judge sentenced Dennis L. Rader to 10 consecutive life terms on Thursday, capping a wrenching hearing in which victims' families, mixing vengeance with grief, confronted the man who had spent decades tormenting them and this city as the strangler called B.T.K.

"I want him to suffer as much as his victims suffered," declared Beverly Plapp, the sister of Nancy Fox, who was 25 when Mr. Rader squeezed the life out of her in 1977. "This man needs to be thrown in a deep, dark hole and left to rot."

Carmen Montoya, whose parents and two younger siblings were Mr. Rader's first victims, in 1974, stared at him and fairly hissed: "You are such a coward."

Mr. Rader, the Cub Scout leader and church council president who nicknamed himself in missives to the news media "B.T.K.," for his bind-torture-kill methods, was not eligible for the death penalty. Judge Greg Waller of Sedgwick County Court imposed the most severe sentence possible, including the so-called hard 40 years without the possibility of parole for the final murder, that of Dolores Davis in 1991, deeming it particularly "heinous, atrocious or cruel."

District Attorney Nola Foulston, the lead prosecutor, said Mr. Rader, 60, would certainly die in prison, with the sentences lining up like boxcars to prevent parole for 175 years.

His ankles in shackles — though not nearly as tight as his victims' — Mr. Rader, who had pleaded guilty and provided an exhaustive confession to the police, removed his glasses to wipe several tears as a dozen relatives of his victims chastised him for a total of 40 minutes. Most of

Dennis L. Rader, center, is escorted into the El Dorado Correctional Facility in El Dorado, Kan. He was sentenced to 10 life terms for murders he committed over nearly 30 years.

them left the courtroom as he rose to deliver his own meandering mono-logue, saying he had been selfish and dishonest, but hoped now to "start a new chapter in my life" and that "someday God will accept me."

In a surreal speech, Mr. Rader read notes from yellow legal paper about what he had in common with his victims: like Kathryn Bright, he spent time on a grandparent's farm; Dolores Davis shared his love for dogs; he and Marine Hedge were both gardeners; Joseph Otero was a fellow veteran of the Air Force.

"She liked to write poetry — I liked to write poetry," he said of Mr. Otero's 11-year-old daughter, Josephine, in a macabre reminder of the depraved poems and sketches the police found in his home. "She liked to draw, I liked to draw."

Mr. Rader quoted Scripture and made a few corrections to the evidence presented by prosecutors. He thanked lawyers, police officers and prison guards as though accepting an award. He asked to retrieve personal photographs from his wallet.

And, finally, he apologized to his victims' families, saying, "There's no way that I can ever repay them."

The sentence came after an extraordinary two-day hearing in which prosecutors and police officers clinically chronicled Mr. Rader's gruesome career in a sort of mini-trial broadcast live on local television and national cable channels. In addition to the maximum sentence, prosecutors urged the judge to recommend restrictive prison conditions that would deny Mr. Rader access to magazines and news-papers, or even crayons and paper, to prevent him from using pictures of girls and women to stimulate himself sexually. Judge Waller said he would decide that in 30 days.

Among the evidence presented Thursday were index cards and three-ring binders containing cutouts of girls and women, includ-ing actresses like Halle Berry and Meg Ryan, from magazines and catalogs. Also seized by the police were lewd Polaroids of Mr. Rad-er's "self-bondage" in his victims' clothing, an extensive collection of Barbie-style dolls he would paint and pose in sexual positions, and books on serial killers, one subtitled "The Methods and Madness of Monsters" that had a mention of B.T.K. highlighted.

Mrs. Foulston made her own dramatic display to demonstrate the horror of Mrs. Davis's death. Noting that Mr. Rader said he had held pantyhose tight around Mrs. Davis's neck for two to three minutes, Mrs. Foulston fell silent, staring at the courtroom clock. She took a sip of water and waited, the only sounds the clicking of a lone photographer's camera and Judge Waller drumming his fingers on his desk.

"One minute has passed," she said finally. "So three times that length was the length of time in which Dolores Davis struggled for her life."

But after hours of detail about the crimes, it was the emotional speeches from the victims' relatives that made Mr. Rader's legacy clear.

They called him monster, devil, predator, pedophile, "rabid animal," "social malignancy" and worse. They shook with anger and sobbed in agony. They spoke of missing sisters, aunts, wives, mothers and grandmothers.

"Every day is a struggle to get through without her," said Stephanie Clyne, who was 10 when her mother, Vicki Wegerle, was killed in 1986. Displaying snapshots of three smiling toddlers on the courtroom screen, Ms. Clyne added, "It's not fair that her three grandbabies never get to see her."

Jeff Davis, the son of Mr. Rader's final victim, said that he had been waiting 5,326 days to "confront the walking cesspool" and that "there could be no justice harsh enough or pain bitter enough."

"This world would have been much better off had your mother aborted your demon soul," Mr. Davis spat. "You have now lost everything, and you will forever remain nothing. May that torment you for the rest of your tortured existence."

Ms. Plapp noted that Mr. Rader had jotted in his vast journals fantasies of how each victim might serve him in the afterlife.

"I have an afterlife concept for him," she said. "On the day that he dies, Nancy and all of his victims will be waiting with God and watching him as he burns in hell."

The Serial Killer's Co-Author

BY RACHEL SHTEIR | SEPT. 15, 2016

BY THE TIME Katherine Ramsland and I stopped at the Copper Oven Cafe and Bakery in the Indian Hills Shopping Center in Wichita, Kan., it was well past lunchtime. It was June 2015, and Ramsland, a professor of forensic psychology and prolific author, was in this sedate city to wind up the last bit of research on "Confession of a Serial Killer," her book about Dennis Rader, which was published this month by University Press of New England. She wore jean capris and a T-shirt and carried a favorite handbag, made of a soft black cloth and decorated with skulls.

That morning, we had begun a tour of the seven places where Rader murdered his 10 victims, the so-called kill sites. Ramsland had already had one final look at the stash of thousands of pieces of Rader's correspondence that Jim Thompson, the lawyer representing the victims' families, kept in his office. She was still hoping to get clearance to visit Rader, now 70, in El Dorado Maximum Security Prison, where he has been serving 10 consecutive life sentences since his arrest in 2005.

At the Copper Oven Cafe, the petite 62-year-old grew tired of my questions about why she studied these horrifying crimes. She reached across the table, grabbed my notebook and quickly sketched the two hands in Michelangelo's "Creation of Adam." She spun the notebook around and pointed to the space between them. She was "interested in everything that is unseen," she said.

What Ramsland, the director of the master's program in criminal justice at DeSales University, means by "unseen" is the near undefinable process by which an apparently ordinary young person, in this case Rader (a.k.a. the "Bind, Torture, Kill" murderer, or "B.T.K."), becomes a serial killer. Although Ramsland regularly talked to Rader on the phone and had corresponded with him for years, she hoped that a visit might provide additional insight into his ghoulish imagination. Later, in an email, she mentioned to me that there was a special "creep factor" to the choice of Copper Oven Cafe as our meeting site: It was right across the street from the house of Vicki Wegerle, whom Rader murdered in 1986. In fact, she informed me, Rader "prepared for the assault in the parking lot," putting on a hard hat to pretend he was a phone repairman.

Rader is famous for how long he evaded capture, living a normal life for three decades before his arrest in 2005. Many books have already been written about the grisly string of crimes he committed in Kansas from 1974 to 1991. But "Confession" stands out as the first that takes the form of a collaboration with the serial killer. Unlike many crime books, it does not merely speculate about a predator's deranged thoughts and schemes but rather plunges the reader into them, revealing in remarkable detail how a well-known serial killer at the end of his life sees himself. Ramsland's rationale in undertaking this unusual project was to overturn what she sees as clichés about serial killers, thereby deglamorizing them and better protecting the public from their depredations. And yet the project raises a host of intellectual and ethical questions — including whether it's possible to uncover the whole truth about these horrifying crimes, and what might be the cost of letting killers tell their own stories.

"He liked these old country roads," Ramsland said cheerfully as her Kia lurched onto a slim dirt strip. She was following a map from The Wichita Eagle showing the locations of the kill sites whose coordinates she had plugged into her GPS device. Blond and fair-skinned, Ramsland dresses in preppy, no-nonsense clothes and talks slowly and sincerely. It was the middle of a hot Kansas afternoon, and a large barn with a silo loomed in a field now framed by bulbous clouds. Such barns, Ramsland said, were a model for his torture lairs. She was also interested in the country bridges, searching for one that looked as it would have in 1991 — country style with wooden beams — to help her understand why Rader was drawn to them. (He dumped the body of a victim under one, and he liked to dress up in bondage gear and suspend himself from them.) But the bridges we saw had been modernized, their beams replaced by cement girders. No good.

Ramsland's career has been an unusual one. In her day job at DeSales, she oversees the master's degree in the criminal-justice program that offers classes in criminology, ethics, forensics, criminal justice and criminal law. But she also has an astonishingly prolific sideline as a popular author, writing some 59 books on a variety of macabre subjects, including ghosts and ghost hunters. In the early 1990s, she broke out with two biographies of genre writers who specialized in depicting fictional monsters: "Prism of the Night," an authorized biography of Anne Rice, and later "Dean Koontz: A Writer's Biography," about the best-selling horror writer. Since then, she has often written multiple nonfiction books per year, a number of them in the true-crime genre, with titles like "Into the Devil's Den" (about an F.B.I. informant who went undercover among white supremacists), "Darkest Waters" (about serial killers in the Great Lakes states) and "The Murder Game" (about murder in Michigan, specifically). She has collaborated with other forensic psychologists and F.B.I. profilers, dug up cold cases, exploited new angles or missed clues.

Even within her oeuvre of murderabilia, "Confession of a Serial Killer" stands out. Composed of roughly 80 percent of Rader's words and 20 percent Ramsland's commentary, it is a murderer's "My Struggle," obsessed with Knausgaardian minutiae, including mistakes in the police report and biographies. One of the book's scoops is that Rader planned to kill many more people than he actually did, and he specifically describes stalking an 11th victim. Equally unsettling, for people familiar with the case, is reading the accounts of the murders Rader committed from his perspective. It has long been believed that he put a chair in the bedroom of one victim, Joseph Otero, purely for the purposes of watching him die; Rader denies this, though he claims not to remember the actual reason, saying it might have been to prevent Otero from "rolling off the bed." Rader also claims that he drank a glass of water in every house in which he killed someone, then cleaned it and put it back in the cupboard. He describes turning up the thermostat in each home, because he read that doing so could impede a medical examiner's attempt to determine a victim's time of death.

The C.S.I.-worthy level of detail makes "Confession" more chilling than the same story told — as it already has been — from the point of view of the heroic cop, the celebrity F.B.I. profiler, the local lawyer, the priest (who believed Rader was possessed), the work colleague unaware of his secret identity or the victim's family member envisioning a conspiracy. Seeing things through Rader's eyes is indeed a stranger vantage point than all of those. The oddness of his language — his fractured diction and superhero jargon (Ramsland includes a glossary) sets it further apart. Serial killers are "Minotaurs." "Factor X" is Rader's drive to kill. "Cubing" is the extreme compartmentaiization that he used to perpetuate his double life. "D.T.P.G." stands for "Death to pretty girls."

Years before she started studying serial killers, Ramsland wrote her Ph.D. dissertation on Soren Kierkegaard, the "father" of existentialism. She sees Kierkegaard as informing her most controversial idea in "Confession" — that some serial killers are more like the rest of us than common wisdom tells us. In the annals of serial killers, Rader is hardly the only one who held down a facade of normalcy while hunting his prey, but he managed it far longer than many others. There are many qualities, Ramsland writes, that ordinary people share with so-called monsters: "overestimating our willpower, idealizing ourselves, daydreaming about power, indulging in secret behaviors that keep attracting us, deceiving others and keeping secrets." She believes that all of us should lock our doors at night.

The strange concept behind "Confession" was hatched in 2010, when Ramsland saw a post on Facebook that Kris Casarona, a self-described accountant and ghostwriter whom Rader had given the media rights to his story, was abandoning the project. Ramsland decided to step in.

By that time, Thompson, the lawyer who represents the victims' families, had rejected a number of writers looking to do some kind of project about him. He told everyone who called to write a proposal of intent, but few followed through. Those who did were not able to win over the families. Ramsland, however, got the go-ahead. The families liked her, Thompson said, though he added that they "didn't really want a book — they would have preferred that he be left in a hole and never heard from again."

Ramsland next had to gain Rader's trust, which she did by writing him a letter expressing her interest and listing her credentials. She apparently impressed him. Soon Ramsland and Rader were corresponding, mostly by mail. "He'll slip into the third person, as Ted Bundy sometimes did," Ramsland said. Sometimes his letters would start with elaborate fake monograms, "From the desk of Dennis Rader." Sometimes he would spend days on a single letter to her. His correspondence could sometimes run to more than 30 pages, composed in a tiny, scratchy hand. They played chess by mail, sending each other their moves. Rader once said, "Don't cheat," Ramsland recalled with a snort, adding in a half-mock-outraged aside: "You're a freakin' serial killer. I'll cheat if I want to!"

When I first met Ramsland, she said her focus on serial killers began somewhat accidentally, in 1998, when she started writing for Crime-Library — a crime website later sold to Court TV — just before she entered John Jay College. But over time, details about her own family's past began to slip out. Her maternal grandfather, she told me, had plotted to poison his wife and children but was caught buying arsenic. Then there was her father's mother, who was murdered by a 20-year old man she was involved with. Ramsland grew up in Saline, Mich., and in 1967, when she was 13, the "Michigan Killer," John Norman Collins, started picking up female hitchhikers in nearby Ann Arbor and stabbing and strangling them; her brother's friends found the remains of one of them in a field. The brother of one of Ramsland's favorite philosophy professors in college, Alfred Dewey Jensen, was murdered by the killer Charles Raymond Starkweather; years later, Jensen killed himself. Violence seemed wound into Ramsland's life as much as — if not more than — Rader's. "Sometimes I wonder if I'm a psychopath," Ramsland said. One question people often ask about this unusual collaboration is whether Rader profits from it. He doesn't, Ramsland explained. In the past 40 years, so-called Son of Sam laws — named after David Berkowitz, who considered selling his story to great outrage in 1977 — have prevented a number of murderers from making money from their stories. In 2005, Thompson worried that Son of Sam laws did not go far enough: They varied from state to state, and a 1991 court ruling had found them to be too broad and possibly unconstitutional. So Thompson and his then co-counsel, Mark Hutton, drew up a contract that gave the families of the victims 75 percent of the profits of all media rights. The current contract, though slightly different, is similarly generous. (Sony has already optioned a TV series.)

Another question "Confession" has raised is about Rader's veracity in his comments and how much it matters whether what he recounts is true. Through her daughter, Rader's ex-wife, Paula Rader, contested two claims Rader makes in the book, particularly his accusation that she knew he was killing people while they were married. And several people who worked on the case have criticized Ramsland for giving Rader a platform, allowing him to portray himself as an evil genius.

Ramsland has responded to these objections by saying that she is seeking to show readers how a serial killer really thinks: lies, exaggerations and all. But she is also acutely aware that Rader — who, from early on, played to the media and tried to exploit it — is looking to make an impression with their book. Although books are not allowed in El Dorado, he has nonetheless been making bookplates to send to pen pals who buy the book. He somehow got a hold of a photo of the cover, which is red, with the title superimposed on a photo of a coil of rope, to suggest strangling, his method of choice. He liked the design.

The day after we visited the kill sites was gloomy and wet. We set out early to see Holcomb, Kan., another site of great interest to true-crime aficionados: It's where Richard Hickock and Perry Smith killed the Clutter family in 1959, forming the basis for Truman Capote's legendary study "In Cold Blood." A teenage Rader became fixated on Hicock and Smith and obsessively read about a host of other historic killers — Albert DeSalvo and Richard Speck, each of whom strangled their victims; Jack the Ripper, who eluded capture; Charles Manson; and the Zodiac Killer.

But Ramsland thinks we're kidding ourselves if we think we can tell the Raders from the civilians just by looking. Rader's outward life was one of normalcy: He served in the Air Force, attended community college, married and had children. He held a variety of jobs — in a supermarket, a factory, for ADT Security Services and the city. He attended Christ Lutheran Church, where he became president of the church council. He was a Cub Scout leader.

I had watched Rader's confession on YouTube, and I liked to think that I would have known he was a psychopath if I met him. He talked about himself in the third person, answering the judge's questions with phrases like "If you know anything about serial killers. ..." As he used the phrase "put him down" to describe killing Joseph Otero, he appeared to be shrugging and twitching; I wondered if he spoke that way ordinarily, and if so, what his wife and children made of it.

When I mentioned my thoughts to Ramsland, though, she disagreed that people who knew Rader could have connected the dots. Why would they? To the contrary, one reason Ramsland believes that Rader was able to keep his cover was that "he grew up in a Germanic Midwestern family where there was not a lot of emotion. Like my family."

We reached Holcomb around noon. We drove by the Valley View Cemetery, stopping briefly to find the Clutter family headstones. Then we headed through town to Oak Street, where the notorious Clutter farmhouse still stood. We parked at the end of the muddy driveway and got out of the car. We could see the two-story building set back on a long, flat parcel of land, the top floor in gray-white siding, the bottom a dull yellow brick. The house seemed so ordinary that it was hard to believe that something so horrible happened there. I looked to see what Ramsland's next move would be, but a do-not-trespass sign discouraged her from going any further. The branches of the Chinese elms bowed as the sky darkened.

CHAPTER 7

The Golden State Killer

The Golden State Killer may have been undone by his DNA. The serial killer, rapist and burglar terrorized northern Californians for 10 years. Between 1976 and 1986, he killed 13 people, raped at least 45 people and burglarized more than 120 homes. And then he stopped. But the police didn't: More than 30 years later, they used a genealogy website to track down distant relatives with DNA profiles that matched the suspect's, leading investigators to arrest Joseph DeAngelo, a 72-year-old former police officer. DeAngelo faces 13 counts of first-degree murder.

Michelle McNamara Hunted, and Was Haunted by, the Golden State Killer

BY ALEXANDRA ALTER | FEB. 15, 2018

THREE DAYS BEFORE she died, Michelle McNamara typed some notes in a cryptic to-do list on her laptop.

Among the looming tasks: "Find out from Debbi D about flashlight." "Find out from Ken exactly what he meant about the husband or the guy in the clown suit walking down the street."

The list cataloged potential clues she planned to chase down as she completed her book, "I'll Be Gone in the Dark," an exhaustive investigation into the identity of the Golden State Killer, who committed upward

After losing his wife, Patton Oswalt couldn't bear the thought of her work languishing.

of 50 sexual assaults and at least 10 murders in California in the 1970s and 1980s.

She never finished it. On April 21, 2016, her husband, the comedian Patton Oswalt, found her dead in the bedroom of their Los Angeles home. An autopsy showed that Ms. McNamara, who was 46, had an undiagnosed heart condition, and had taken a dangerous mix of prescription drugs, including Adderall, the pain narcotic Fentanyl and the anti-anxiety medication Xanax.

The story that she spent the last five years of her life obsessively researching was half written, the gruesome mystery still unsolved. After losing his wife, Mr. Oswalt couldn't bear the thought of her work languishing.

"This book had to be finished," he said in a telephone interview. "Knowing how horrible this guy was, there was this feeling of, you're not going to silence another victim. Michelle died, but her testimony is going to get out there."

Shortly after her death, Mr. Oswalt recruited Billy Jensen, an investigative journalist, and Paul Haynes, who worked closely with Ms. McNamara on the book as a researcher, to comb through her handwritten notes and the roughly 3,500 files on her computer and piece together the story she set out to tell.

"I'll Be Gone in the Dark," due out Feb. 27, is both a vivid and meticulous investigation of a twisted predator who terrorized quiet, upper middle-class communities in California for nearly a decade, and a wrenching personal account from a writer who became consumed by her subject. It's drawn accolades from some of the country's top crime and horror writers, including Stephen King, Michael Connelly, Megan Abbott and Gillian Flynn, who wrote an introduction to the book.

The tragedy of Ms. McNamara's death became a meta-narrative running through the book. Its pages are punctuated with recurring editor's notes that serve as a reminder that the author, who is so palpably present on the page, is absent from the world. She wrote frankly about the psychological toll the project took on her, how immersing herself in the grisly details left her emotionally frayed. "There's a scream permanently lodged in my throat now," Ms. McNamara wrote.

Rather than attempting to mimic her voice and flesh out fragmentary chapters, or condense her sprawling research into a taut true crime narrative, Mr. Haynes and Mr. Jensen let the jagged edges of the unfinished project show. They preserved her completed chapters, which recount the killer's attacks in unsparing detail and examine his methodology, and explore her own fascination with unsolved crimes and her evolution as an amateur detective. Other chapters were pieced together from her notes, and are marked with disclaimers. Some sections read like raw, unfiltered research: one mesmerizing chapter consists entirely of a transcript from Ms. McNamara's interview with Paul Holes, a criminalist in the Contra Costa sheriff's office.

Toward the end of the book, just as Ms. McNamara's investigation seems to be gaining momentum and the killer's hazy profile begins to come into focus, it grinds to a halt. An editor's note explains how, after

Ms. McNamara died, Mr. Haynes and Mr. Jensen were brought in to "tie up loose ends and organize the materials Michelle left behind." In that final section, Mr. Haynes and Mr. Jensen lay out some of the avenues that Ms. McNamara had planned to explore. They describe what they found on her laptop — old maps and aerial photographs of Goleta, the site of multiple murders, images of shoe prints found at crime scenes, and a spreadsheet with names and addresses of men who competed on a 1976 high school cross-country team (she thought the perpetrator might be a runner, based on victims's descriptions of his muscular legs). They explore the potential for using D.N.A. and genealogy databases to identify the killer's family, which Ms. McNamara believed was the best route for finding a criminal who had evaded investigators for four decades.

It took Mr. Haynes and Mr. Jensen about a year to put the book together, and one can feel their frustration at wrestling with all of the evidence and theories that Ms. McNamara compiled, and still coming up empty.

Mr. Haynes, who worked closely with Ms. McNamara for several years, was stunned and devastated by her death, he said. He also had to wrestle with the sweeping territory Ms. McNamara intended to cover.

"It's a very ambitious book to write, about a case like this with a scope as vast as it is," Mr. Haynes said. "The question was, what holes should we attempt to patch?"

Ms. McNamara became fascinated with unsolved crimes when she was growing up in Oak Park, Ill., the youngest of six siblings in a large Irish Catholic family. When Ms. McNamara was 14, a young woman named Kathleen Lombardo was murdered near the McNamaras's home. More curious than afraid, Ms. McNamara went to the alley where the body was found, and picked up shards of the victim's broken Walkman. The killer was never caught.

She was living in Los Angeles and writing screenplays and TV pilots when she met Mr. Oswalt in 2003, at one of his comedy shows. They went on a few dates and bonded over their shared obsession with serial killers. They got married a couple of years later, and Mr. Oswalt urged her to channel her grim hobby into writing. In 2006, she launched her website, True Crime Diary, where she chronicled hundreds of unsolved crimes.

In 2011, she wrote on her blog about a string of unsolved rapes and murders from the 1970s and 1980s that were committed by an unidentified man who was known as the East Area Rapist and the Original Night Stalker. "I'm obsessed," she wrote. "It's not healthy." For a true crime addict, the case was tantalizingly complex. So much was known about his methods and even his psychology, yet the killer had thwarted investigators for decades. He was a meticulous planner who stalked his targets in advance, learning their daily routines before breaking into their homes. He brought his own precut ligatures to tie victims up, and always wore a mask. He stole objects that had sentimental value for the victims, like engraved jewelry and class rings. He grew increasingly confident, and went from assaulting women who were home alone to attacking couples in their bedrooms. She gave him a catchier name: the Golden State Killer.

Ms. McNamara wrote about the case for Los Angeles magazine, and signed a book deal with Harper several months later.

The research consumed her, and began to weigh on her. She suffered from insomnia and anxiety. Once, she panicked because she woke up to a scraping sound: A neighbor was dragging his trash can to the curb in the middle of the night, Mr. Oswalt said. Another time, when Mr. Oswalt tiptoed into their bedroom, trying not to wake her, she mistook him for an intruder and jumped out of bed and swung a lamp at his head. She felt an obligation to solve the case, and was devastated each time she developed a promising theory or zeroed in on a suspect but failed to find sufficient evidence.

"She had overloaded her mind with information with very dark implications," Mr. Oswalt said.

Mr. Oswalt wasn't aware of all the prescriptions she was taking or what the medications were for, he said. Both of them led busy work lives and were devoted parents to their then 7-year-old daughter, Alice, and Ms. McNamara seemed to be managing the stress. It wasn't until he saw the coroner's report months after her death that he realized that Ms. McNamara was coping in part by taking prescription drugs.

"It's so clear that the stress led her to make some bad choices in terms of the pharmaceuticals she was using," he said. "She just took this stuff on, and she didn't have the years of being a hardened detective to compartmentalize it."

Mr. Oswalt, who married the actress Meredith Salenger last year, said he still thinks there's a chance the killer will eventually be caught, due in part to the work Ms. McNamara did and the attention it brought to a decades old cold case.

Ms. McNamara believed that too. In a letter to the killer that appears at the end of "I'll Be Gone in the Dark," she addresses him directly, and says it's only a matter of time until officers arrive at his door. "This is how it ends for you," she writes.

Search for 'Golden State Killer' Leads to Arrest of Ex-Cop

BY THOMAS FULLER AND CHRISTINE HAUSER | APRIL 25, 2018

SACRAMENTO — It was a rash of sadistic rapes and murders that spread terror throughout California, long before the term was commonly used. The scores of attacks in the 1970s and 1980s went unsolved for more than three decades. But on Wednesday, law enforcement officials said they had finally arrested the notorious Golden State Killer in a tidy suburb of Sacramento.

Joseph James DeAngelo, 72, who was taken into custody outside his home on Tuesday and charged with six counts of murder, had been living undisturbed a half-hour drive from where the 12-year rampage began. He was described as a former police officer, and his time in uniform partly overlapped with many of the crimes he is accused of committing.

The case was cracked in the past week, Sheriff Scott Jones of Sacramento County said on Wednesday, when investigators identified Mr. DeAngelo and were able to match his DNA with the murders of Lyman and Charlene Smith in Ventura County in 1980.

"We found the needle in the haystack and it was right here in Sacramento," said Anne Marie Schubert, the Sacramento district attorney, who helped organize a task force two years ago that included investigators from across the state as well as the F.B.I. A DNA database showed links to other murders in Southern California, the authorities said Wednesday.

A series of rapes in an old gold mining area east of Sacramento in 1976 were first linked by the authorities for their geographic proximity, the similar description of the rapist — a white male with blond hair who was just under six feet tall — and the peculiar and cruel rituals that he inflicted on his victims. His victims included women home alone and women at home with their children. The suspect went on to rape women with their husbands present and then murder them both.

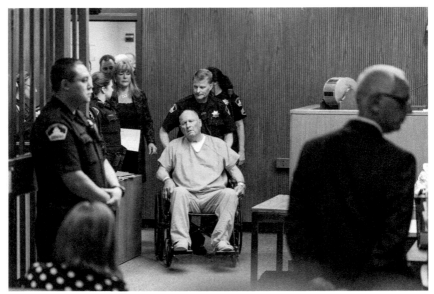

Joseph James DeAngelo, 72, was arrested at a home in Citrus Heights, Calif.

He is also thought to have burglarized more than 120 homes.

He became an infamous figure, sometimes known as the Golden State Killer and other times as the East Area Rapist and the Original Night Stalker. His planning was meticulous and he seemed to know precise details about his victims' schedules. They described the gravelly, angry whisper that he used as he tormented them. He wore gloves and a mask and was a predator with quirks: As his victims lay terrified, he would pause for a snack of crackers after raping them. He placed a teacup and saucer on the bodies of some of his victims and threatened them with murder if he heard the ceramic rattle.

With communities panicking — at one point his assaults averaged two victims a month — the authorities hired a range of experts to help them break the case, among them a military special forces officer and a psychic.

Then, when the rapes and murders appeared to end in 1986, the case went cold.

National interest was reignited this year with the publication of an exhaustive investigation into the serial killer's identity, "I'll Be Gone in the Dark," written by Michelle McNamara, a crime writer who died in April 2016. The book, published in February, was completed after her death by a journalist and researcher recruited by her husband, the comedian Patton Oswalt.

Mr. Oswalt spoke about the reported capture on Wednesday in a video posted on Instagram. "I think you got him, Michelle," he said.

Mr. DeAngelo, whom the authorities suspect of committing a total of 12 murders, was arrested by investigators using some of the same tactics employed by the suspect to stalk his victims — the police surveilled his movements, studied his routines and pounced when he left his house.

He was arrested on a warrant stemming from the murder of the married couple in Ventura County in Southern California, but the authorities said more charges were in the works. The Orange County district attorney's office announced four additional charges late on Wednesday.

Residents of the neighborhoods stalked by the killer said he changed the way they lived their lives. A carefree California lifestyle of open doors and children riding their bicycles to school was forever changed with the knowledge that a rapist now lurked.

"One person can create a lot of fear," said Tony Rackauckas, the district attorney of Orange County and one of the dozens of officials on hand in Sacramento to announce Mr. DeAngelo's arrest. "It was like terrorism — not that it was done for the same reason — but it caused the same type of fear."

The case had a profound impact not just on fear and public safety in California, but also on the way that rapes were investigated and how rape victims were treated, said Carol Daly, a detective in the Sacramento County Sheriff's Office at the time.

Locks sold out at hardware stores and over 6,000 guns were sold, she said. Community safety forums would be packed with hundreds of people.

Rape victims were seen and cared for faster, and pubic hair, scratches and other evidence were examined and preserved, she said. Rape kits were standardized. "Every victim went through the process," she said.

Bruce Harrington, whose brother Keith Harrington and sister-in-law Patrice Harrington were among the murder victims, joined law enforcement officers at the news conference. It was "time for the victims to begin to heal," he said.

"Sleep better tonight, he isn't coming in through the window," he said. "He's now in jail, and he's history."

One victim, Jane Carson-Sandler, who was raped in 1976, said on Wednesday that she was overwhelmed with emotion.

Ms. Carson-Sandler, 72, said she had always believed that her rapist was alive and that he would be caught. The hatred and anger she felt eventually faded, she said, but she continued to pray for two things each night: that he would be identified, and that she wouldn't dream about the rape.

She never did dream about it, she said, and on Wednesday morning she turned on her phone to learn that a suspect had been arrested.

"I just feel so blessed that God has finally answered all of our prayers, that this monster would eventually be put behind bars," she said.

Mr. DeAngelo, who has adult children, was twice employed as a police officer in two small California cities: In Exeter, in the Central Valley, from 1973 to 1976, and in Auburn, north of Sacramento, from 1976 to 1979, according to Mr. Jones.

He was convicted in 1979 for shoplifting a can of dog repellent and a hammer from a store in Sacramento County. The incident led to his dismissal from the Auburn police force. The arrest came amid the rash of rapes in the area.

One of the neighborhoods where the suspect repeatedly struck was Rancho Cordova, a Sacramento suburb of ranch houses, redwood and birch trees, trim lawns and rose bushes.

In one attack in 1978, Brian and Katie Maggiore, a couple living in the area, were walking their dog in their neighborhood around 9 p.m.

After a "violent encounter" with the suspect, they tried to flee, ending up in a private yard, where they were fatally shot, the sheriff's department said in February, appealing to the public for leads.

Diane Peterson, a retired teacher who lives in Rancho Cordova, said Wednesday that theories about who was behind the rapes and home intrusions had remained a topic of conversation in the neighborhood in the four decades since the attacks began.

"It never totally died down," Ms. Peterson said. "People would have their own suspicions as to who it might be."

Jean McNeill, a retired employee for the state board of equalization who lives near where one of the murders took place, said she was "elated" Wednesday morning when she heard that the suspect might have been captured.

She remembered the terror that the killer instilled in the neighborhood.

"I can remember thinking, 'It's getting dark and no one is home with me — I've got to be really careful,' " she said. "That's what made it so frightening. We didn't know when he was going to strike next."

After the Maggiore murders, the attacker was not believed to have struck in the Sacramento area again. But in 2001, investigators using DNA evidence linked the crime to others committed in the Bay Area, and to murders in Southern California, the sheriff's department said.

In June 2016, the F.B.I. announced at a news conference that it would offer a $50,000 reward for information leading to the arrest and conviction of the "prolific serial rapist and murderer."

"We came together to bring solace to the victims," Sean Ragan, special agent in charge of the Sacramento office for the F.B.I., said Wednesday. "But we know the pain and anguish has never subsided."

THOMAS FULLER reported from Sacramento and CHRISTINE HAUSER from New York. ADAM GOLDMAN contributed reporting from Washington, and DANIEL VICTOR and RICHARD A. OPPEL JR. from New York.

What We Know About Joseph DeAngelo, the Golden State Killer Suspect

BY MATTHEW HAAG | APRIL 26, 2018

FROM 1976 TO 1986, one man struck fear in the hearts of Californians from Sacramento to San Francisco to Los Angeles, killing 12 people, raping at least 45 people and burglarizing more than 120 homes in meticulously planned crimes.

He was known by many names: the Golden State Killer, the East Area Rapist, the Diamond Knot Killer and the Original Night Stalker. But until last week, decades of detective work had not uncovered the name of Joseph James DeAngelo.

A statewide hunt for the suspect finally ended on Tuesday, when the authorities said that they had arrested Mr. DeAngelo, 72, and that he was responsible for the series of murders and rapes. In the end, the decades-long hunt for the infamous figure ended not far from where the case started. Here's what we know so far about the suspect.

He was a former cop who served in the Navy. The Golden State Killer usually struck at night after carefully planning his attack, even down to the smallest details, ahead of time. He studied his victims' schedules, broke into their homes and unlocked windows or removed screens in preparation for his return. He turned off porch lights and hid shoelaces and ropes to use later to bind his victims.

In one attack, he hid in a couple's closet, waited for them to fall asleep and then announced himself, shining a flashlight on them, according to a retired Sacramento County sheriff's deputy. When the husband reached for a gun next to him in bed, the attacker flashed the light on the bullets he was holding. He had already emptied the gun.

A photo of Joseph James DeAngelo was displayed at a news conference in Sacramento announcing his arrest.

His patience, reconnaissance and ability to escape manhunts, as well as the intricate knots he used to bind victims, led detectives to believe he had served in the military or in law enforcement. Mr. DeAngelo did both.

He served in the Navy during the Vietnam War, working as a damage control man aboard a warship, the Canberra, according to a June 1967 article in The Auburn Journal in Auburn, Calif., where his parents lived.

From 1973 to 1976, Mr. DeAngelo was an officer with the Exeter Police Department in Exeter, Calif., a small city about 50 miles southeast of Fresno.

In 1976, the same year as the first attack, Mr. DeAngelo joined the Auburn Police Department, about 20 miles northeast of Sacramento.

Nicholas Willick was a patrol sergeant with the Auburn police when Mr. DeAngelo joined the force. Mr. Willick recalled that at the time, the department's 17 or so officers handled mostly property crimes.

But it was also a time of heightened alarm in Northern California, as a series of brutal murders had rocked the region.

In an interview on his front porch in Auburn on Thursday, Mr. Willick said he never suspected that Mr. DeAngelo might have been responsible for those killings.

What Mr. Willick recalls about Mr. DeAngelo was a small quirk — he'd lost part of a finger, something that he'd told the department happened in Vietnam.

Other than that, there was little remarkable about Mr. DeAngelo, Mr. Willick said. He seemed like many of the other officers, and even gave some of his colleagues an informal tour of his new home — like the proud newlywed that he was. "He was just an average person, an average Joe."

Until, of course, a local police department called in 1979 to say Mr. DeAngelo had been caught stealing dog repellant and a hammer from a drugstore. By then, Mr. Willick had become the Auburn police chief. "I fired him," Mr. Willick said. "He violated the law."

After that, Mr. DeAngelo's law enforcement career ended and Mr. Willick never saw him again — until his name and face surfaced in the news as the man suspected of being the Golden State Killer.

On his porch, in a white wicker chair, Mr. Willick said he was both embarrassed that Mr. DeAngelo had gone free for so long, and sure that he could have done nothing to stop him.

"Anytime, my goodness, you know, the person was a police officer, it's an embarrassment to law enforcement — not just an embarrassment to me," he said.

But, he added, "anything that would say that this person was a vicious murderer, a serial rapist? No, nothing whatsoever, no indications, and that's probably why the joint task force has worked 40-some-odd years to solve this case."

He lived near where many of the attacks took place. When the authorities announced the arrest of Mr. DeAngelo on Tuesday, they said they had long believed the case would end near where it started. He lived with his daughter and granddaughter, according to KTVU-TV in Oakland, in a home in Citrus Heights, a city northeast of Sacramento.

The first 15 attacks occurred in the Sacramento area, including four in Citrus Heights. Not until 1978, after at least 30 attacks, were crimes committed outside that area.

The F.B.I. and local authorities were seen removing items from Mr. DeAngelo's home on Wednesday. Neighbors said that he was meticulous — he mowed his lawn to exacting detail — and that he was prone to outbursts and yelling curse words. "He liked the F word a lot," one neighbor told The Associated Press.

He was engaged to one woman and married another. When Mr. DeAngelo was 24, he was engaged to a woman who lived in Auburn, Bonnie Jean Colwell, according to an announcement in The Auburn Journal. They both attended Sierra College, a community college in Northern California. But they did not marry.

In 1973, Mr. DeAngelo, then 27, married Sharon Huddle, who was 20 at the time and lived in Citrus Heights. Sharon Huddle DeAngelo, a lawyer, went on to help found the National Coalition Against Surrogacy, a Washington group started in 1987 that pushed for legislation to outlaw surrogacy.

Her brother, James Huddle, told Oxygen.com on Wednesday that the couple raised three daughters but separated at some point. Mr. Huddle said he was stunned by Mr. DeAngelo's arrest, but said Mr. DeAngelo once brought up the Golden State Killer case in a conversation with him.

He retired from the grocery business last year. For 27 years, Mr. DeAngelo worked at a distribution center for the grocery store Save Mart, the company told The Sacramento Bee, before he retired in 2017. The distribution center is in Roseville, a suburb of Sacramento.

It is unclear where Mr. DeAngelo worked from 1979, when he left the Auburn Police Department, to the early 1990s, when he joined Save

Mart. "None of his actions in the workplace would have led us to suspect any connection to crimes being attributed to him," a Save Mart spokesman told The Sacramento Bee.

DNA connected the cases and led to his arrest. Before 2001, detectives in California knew there had been a string of unsolved murders and rapes in Southern California and a set of attacks in Northern California. But a criminalist in Contra Costa County finally linked the two sets of cases to the same man in 2001, thanks to DNA evidence and new technology.

And it was DNA that led detectives to Mr. DeAngelo last week. The authorities have not said how they first became aware of him. But last week, they surveilled him and surreptitiously collected his DNA from two items he had discarded, law enforcement officials said on Wednesday.

The results came back as a match to the Golden State Killer cases, and he was finally arrested.

JULIE TURKEWITZ contributed reporting from Auburn, Calif. SUSAN C. BEACHY contributed research.

Do Serial Killers Just Stop? Yes, Sometimes

BY JAN HOFFMAN | APRIL 26, 2018

THE GOLDEN STATE KILLER'S barrage of rapes and murders began in a gold mining area east of Sacramento in 1976. By 1986, it seemed to have stopped.

Why?

With the arrest Tuesday of Joseph James DeAngelo, 72, who has been charged so far with eight counts of murder, more than 30 years had passed since the last episode in the series. That long period of quiescence seems to fly in the face of the popular belief that serial rapists and killers are incapable of stopping.

But forensic psychiatrists, criminal profilers and homicide detectives who pursue cold cases say that assumption is more myth than reality.

"These are not acts that a person is compelled to do," said J. Reid Meloy, a forensic psychologist and professor of psychiatry at the University of California, San Diego. "They are intentional and predatory. There is choice, capacity and opportunity that is exercised."

Any number of factors can contribute to a dormant stretch. An extensive 2008 study on serial murder for the F.B.I.'s National Center for the Analysis of Violent Crime found that killers may quiet down when they find other outlets for their emotions. The study mentioned Dennis Rader, known as the BTK Killer, who murdered 10 people from 1974 to 1991, but had no other victims before being apprehended in 2005. "During interviews conducted by law enforcement, Rader admitted to engaging in autoerotic activities as a substitute for his killings," the report said.

Other killers might have changed behavior after moving away from the original epicenter of activity. Ted Bundy mutilated and murdered perhaps more than 30 young women in the 1970s. Yet there were stretches along his peripatetic travels when he was not associated with murders in those areas.

In some cases, jobs and families might have stabilized and exacerbating sources of stress might have faded, some experts said.

Dr. Michael H. Stone, a professor of forensic psychiatry at Columbia University who has extensively studied serial killers, noted that Gary Ridgeway, the Green River Killer, murdered prostitutes during his first two difficult marriages. He married a third time, more happily, and the killings dwindled.

"Some of these men have little oases of compassion, within the vast desert of their contempt and hatred of women," Dr. Stone said.

So far, the authorities have not offered any public explanation as to why the Golden State Killer spree, for which Mr. DeAngelo was arrested this week, began and continued, much less stopped. But some experts point to the most banal explanation: In 1986, when he was 40, Mr. DeAngelo may have aged out.

"The testosterone levels are down," Dr. Stone said. "His capacity to perform is weakened," he added, noting that he was merely speculating. The prey drive is lessened.

Mark Safarik, a retired F.B.I. criminal profiler and consultant to crime shows like "Bones" and "The Blacklist," recently worked on a study with academic researchers about older sexual homicide offenders. "They are really rare over age 50," he said. "We just don't see them. Pedophiles over 50, yes. But not rape-murderers."

There is little research on why spree killers desist for reasons other than getting caught. No one knows what has happened to a serial killer of young women on Long Island.

"There has never been a survey of serial killers asking them why they stopped," said Eric Witzig, a retired homicide detective and chairman of the Murder Accountability Project, a database of unsolved murders. "All we have are anecdotal hunches," he said.

Perhaps a victim struggled and spooked the attacker, he said. The killer "might think then, 'Maybe I don't want to do this anymore because I might get caught.' Or, 'I want to stop and reflect on the carnage I wreaked in the past.' "

Or, said Dr. Bruce E. Harry, a retired forensic psychiatrist with the University of Missouri medical school: "Maybe they get tired or bored and just don't want to do it anymore."

Mr. Safarik, the retired F.B.I. crime profiler, was a beat cop in the late 1970s in Davis, Calif. and remembers being on stakeouts for the Golden State Killer, watching with night surveillance scopes for a man scrambling over rooftops or escaping into nearby fields.

Then, as now, police believed that the suspect had military or law enforcement training, which helped him evade detection. One reason the rapist-murderer may have stopped in the late 80s, speculated Mr. Safarik, is that he was becoming aware of the ability to collect DNA evidence, left by the most meager material. The public was becoming familiar with it, he said, particularly through television dramas.

Several experts, underlining the notion that so little is yet known about Mr. DeAngelo — including most significantly whether he committed the crimes — wondered whether the criminal behavior did stop entirely in 1986.

"I would want to look at other rapes and murders in the areas where he lived over time," Dr. Meloy said. "I would be skeptical that there was a complete shutdown at age 40."

The Golden State Killer Left a Trail of Horror With Taunts and Guile

BY DAN BARRY, TIM ARANGO AND RICHARD A. OPPEL JR. | APRIL 28, 2018

SACRAMENTO — Throughout 1977, the terrified residents of Sacramento County wanted to know when their horror movie of an existence would end. In packed community forums, they expressed their fears about the sadistic predator who was committing sexual assaults in their previously tranquil neighborhoods every few days — someone nicknamed the East Area Rapist.

At one gathering, in a school cafeteria, a Sacramento sheriff's detective named Carol Daly gave a brief tutorial about defending oneself against the attacker. But before the few hundred audience members dispersed into the California night, a man questioned how anyone could possibly get away with raping a woman in the presence of her husband, who would do everything in his power to prevent an assault.

A few months later, the East Area Rapist targeted that very man and his wife, in one of the more brutal attacks of the dozens he had committed. Ms. Daly, now retired, said on Friday that she has no doubt:

"The rapist was there at that meeting."

The horrifying moment reflected how the meticulous criminal — whom investigators strongly suspected had law enforcement connections — taunted his pursuers with catch-me-if-you-can brio. He was flaunting his power, it seemed, as well as his belief that he could elude accountability forever.

He was wrong.

On Tuesday morning, Joseph James DeAngelo, 72, was a retiree and former police officer, known to his neighbors as an occasional crank obsessed with lawn care. By that night, he had been arrested as the suspected East Area Rapist, a.k.a. the Original Night Stalker, a.k.a. the Diamond Knot Killer — a.k.a. the Golden State Killer.

JASON HENRY FOR THE NEW YORK TIMES

Neighbors watch as law enforcement and media line the usually quiet street where Joseph James DeAngelo lived in Citrus Heights, Calif.

The widely disseminated mug shot of the older, balding DeAngelo, juxtaposed beside a decades-old police sketch of a young suspect with longish hair parted in the middle, twinned the distance of the long-ago with the immediacy of now.

Beyond Sacramento, that year of 1977 unfolded apace: a new president named Jimmy Carter; a hot movie called "Star Wars"; the death of Elvis. But in and around the capital city of California, reports of yet another horrific attack by the East Area Rapist overshadowed everyday life, becoming the obsession of, among others, Detective Daly.

The first occurred in June 1976. Then another in July, in August, in September. After several more in October, law enforcement officials announced that they were looking for one perpetrator tied to attack after attack. He came to be known as the East Area Rapist.

"The fear in the community was like something I had never seen before," said Ms. Daly, who was part of a task force dedicated to the case. "People were afraid wherever they went."

With good reason.

The rapist typically wore a ski mask, and usually wielded a gun. He tied up his victims, and issued threatening instructions through clenched teeth. He took mementos: photographs, jewelry, identification. He sometimes paused to eat or drink, as if to suggest he was perfectly at home with mayhem.

The attacks were devastating to women and their families. But Linda O'Dell, one of the victims, recalled Ms. Daly's deftness, at a time when victims of rape were often re-victimized by the law enforcement procedures that followed. "She was a trailblazer," Ms. O'Dell said of the detective. "She was very comforting to me."

Investigators soon developed an outline of their suspect: an agile young man, just under 6 feet tall and with a size-9 shoe, whose tactical precision suggested military or law enforcement experience. He was also particularly audacious: After a local newspaper noted that he raped his victims when no man was at home, Ms. Daly recalled, he began assaulting women while tying up their husbands.

"He was so in tune with what we were doing and what was in the media," she said. "And every time we would say, 'Well, he didn't do this,' it was: 'Ha-ha. I gotcha. I could do it.'"

This calculated audacity fed into the suspicion that, at the very least, the perpetrator had had law enforcement training.

"At the time," Ms. Daly said, "it was a strong enough suspicion that he could have been law enforcement that all of the men in our department who matched his description came forward and got themselves eliminated," through blood tests matched with a sample of the rapist's blood.

Monica Miller, the head of the Sacramento F.B.I. field office from 2013 to 2017, agreed that the predator's patterns suggested that he either knew what police would look for at a crime scene or had inside information into the investigation.

"He was extremely wily," Ms. Miller said. "Just the way he was able to elude the U.S. He was smarter than the average person when it came to tactics or techniques."

The rapist flashed his boldness again after that community forum at which the audience member expressed his doubt that a woman could be attacked with a man in the house. And the subsequent assault on his wife, Ms. Daly recalled, was especially savage.

"They were all savage," she said. "But he just seemed to have spent more time in that home, with repeated assaults. I think he was thumbing his nose at everybody."

At this time, Mr. DeAngelo was a police officer in Auburn, a community tucked into the Northern California foothills, not far from where he had attended high school. He wore the light blue uniform, patrolled the quaint streets, and responded to routine calls — all while the residents of Auburn were being rattled by reports of the serial attacker called the East Area Rapist.

Nicholas Willick, an Auburn police officer who served with Mr. DeAngelo and who later became police chief, recalled the tenor of the time, with people installing alarm systems, packing handguns and buying guard dogs.

"We were getting besieged with phone calls wanting an officer to come over to the house to make security checks and make suggestions on how they could make their houses more safe," Mr. Willick recalled. "Because people were afraid."

In February 1978, a married couple, Brian and Katie Maggiore, were shot to death while walking their dog in the Sacramento County city of Rancho Cordova. This, it would turn out, would be the first murder linked to the East Area Rapist.

The next year, in early July, Chief Willick fired Mr. DeAngelo from the police force after he was arrested for trying to steal a hammer and a can of dog repellent from a Pay 'n Save store by concealing them in his trousers.

Three months later, the serial rapist tied up a couple in Goleta, a city near Santa Barbara, nearly 400 miles south of Sacramento. He fled on a bicycle after the woman began screaming.

The next month, in November, Mr. DeAngelo took the stand to deny that he was trying to steal the items. Found guilty, he was given a $100 fine and six months' probation.

The rapes and murders continued for years, in California locations far beyond Sacramento County. All the while, Ms. Daly retained a large red binder packed with reports and photos and interviews — a resource she often shared with investigators who came after her.

"This is something that, once it's been with you, it does not leave you," she said.

In 1986, the predator's 12-year spree of break-ins, violence and death stopped — at least, it seems, in California. Twelve dead, at least 50 women raped, and more than 120 homes burglarized.

The reasons remain unclear. Ms. Daly surmised that the killer had lost his agility to outrun police officers, or perhaps had come so close to getting caught that he decided to stop. "I felt that something happened that he just wasn't able to do those crimes anymore," she said.

Interest in the case waxed and waned over the decades. In 2001, advancements in DNA technology led to the establishment of a link between rapes in Northern California and murders in Southern California. In 2013, the crime writer Michelle McNamara shined a spotlight on the case with an article in Los Angeles magazine. And in 2016, the F.B.I. and the Sacramento County district attorney's office announced a renewed effort to solve it.

Mr. DeAngelo and his wife had three daughters, but at some point the couple separated. He worked for more than a quarter-century at a distribution center for the Save Mart grocery store chain in Roseville, outside of Sacramento. He retired in 2017 and was noticed, if at all, for his painstaking lawn care, and for occasional outbursts of obscenity.

Then, on Tuesday, the police came for a fallen member of their fraternity. Ms. Daly, long-retired, was among those who got a heads-up call, and 40 years of emotions welled up.

Mr. DeAngelo had his wrists shackled to his government-issue wheelchair on Friday at his arraignment in Sacramento.

"It's been borderline tears from the time I got the phone call," she said. Late last year, law enforcement officials had uploaded the suspect's DNA profile, culled from the scene of a 1980 double murder in Ventura County, to a website dedicated to genealogy. That approach was a Hail Mary from Paul Holes, an investigator with the Contra Costa County district attorney's office who had worked the case for 24 years and was about to retire.

Four months of sleuthing on the genealogy website led to distant relatives of Mr. DeAngelo, and from there genealogists helped pinpoint Mr. DeAngelo himself — whose DNA, taken from items he discarded outside his home, was a match with the killer's, according to the police.

On Friday afternoon, Mr. DeAngelo was rolled into a Sacramento County courtroom, his wrists shackled to his government-issued wheelchair. He wore an orange jumpsuit with "Sacramento Co Prisoner" stenciled in large letters on the back.

Judge Michael W. Sweet ascertained, after some difficulty, that the defendant's name was Joseph James DeAngelo. He then recited the charges, including the murder of Katie Maggiore — "a human being" — and of Brian Maggiore — "a human being."

The former police officer gazed at the judge, blinking slowly and with his mouth partly open, as if there were no words. Then he was wheeled away.

TIM ARANGO reported from Sacramento, and **DAN BARRY** and **RICHARD A. OPPEL JR.** from New York. Reporting was contributed by **THOMAS FULLER** from Sacramento; **JULIE TURKEWITZ** from Auburn, Calif.; **JENNIFER MEDINA** and **JOSE A. DEL REAL** from Los Angeles; and **ADAM GOLDMAN** from Washington.

Glossary

cannibalism The practice of eating human flesh.

indictment The formal accusation of a crime.

jurisprudence The science or philosophy of law.

monomaniac Term used in 19th-century psychiatry to describe a person with a single pathological obsession but who is otherwise thought to be sane.

necrophilia Sex with or sexual attraction to corpses.

paranoiac A person who suffers from paranoia, a mental condition characterized by grandiose self-importance, delusions of persecution or baseless jealousy.

paretic Partial paralysis.

parricide Murder of one's father, mother or other close relative.

peremptorily challenged A lawyer's challenge of a prospective juror for which no reason needs to be provided.

perpetrator A person who commits a harmful, violent or illegal act.

streetwalker A prostitute.

stringer A journalist who works part-time for a newspaper.

sweat box A narrow prison cell or box in which a prisoner is placed for punishment.

talesman Archaic term for bystander selected to join a jury to make up a deficit in the required number of jurors.

tenuous Weak or insubstantial.

Media Literacy Terms

"Media literacy" refers to the ability to access, understand, critically assess and create media. The following terms are important components of media literacy, and they will help you critically engage with the articles in this title.

angle The aspect of a news story on which a journalist focuses and develops.

attribution The method by which a source is identified or by which facts and information are assigned to the person who provided them.

balance Principle of journalism that both perspectives of an argument should be presented in a fair way.

chronological order Method of writing a story presenting the details of the story in the order in which they occurred.

commentary Type of story that is an expression of opinion on recent events by a journalist generally known as a commentator.

credibility The quality of being trustworthy and believable, said of a journalistic source.

critical review Type of story that describes an event or work of art, such as a theater performance, film, concert, book, restaurant, radio or television program, exhibition or musical piece, and offers critical assessment of its quality and reception.

editorial Article of opinion or interpretation.

feature story Article designed to entertain as well as to inform.

headline Type, usually 18 point or larger, used to introduce a story.

human interest story Type of story that focuses on individuals and how events or issues affect their lives, generally offering a sense of relatability to the reader.

impartiality Principle of journalism that a story should not reflect a journalist's bias and should contain balance.

intention The motive or reason behind something, such as the publication of a news story.

interview story Type of story in which the facts are gathered primarily by interviewing another person or persons.

motive The reason behind something, such as the publication of a news story or a source's perspective on an issue.

news story An article or style of expository writing that reports news, generally in a straightforward fashion and without editorial comment.

op-ed An opinion piece that reflects a prominent individual's opinion on a topic of interest.

paraphrase The summary of an individual's words, with attribution, rather than a direct quotation of their exact words.

quotation The use of an individual's exact words indicated by the use of quotation marks and proper attribution.

reliability The quality of being dependable and accurate, said of a journalistic source.

rhetorical device Technique in writing intending to persuade the reader or communicate a message from a certain perspective.

source The origin of the information reported in journalism.

style A distinctive use of language in writing or speech; also a news or publishing organization's rules for consistent use of language with regards to spelling, punctuation, typography and capitalization, usually regimented by a house style guide.

tone A manner of expression in writing or speech.

Media Literacy Questions

1. What is the intention of the article "The London Paranoiac." (on page 17)? How effectively does the article achieve this purpose?

2. Does the writer demonstrate the journalistic principle of impartiality in the article "The Case Opened." (on page 37)? If so, how? If not, what could have been included to make the article more impartial?

3. What type of story is "Suspect Is Emerging as a Study in Extreme and Varied Contrast" (on page 79)? Can you identify another article in this collection that is the same type of story? What elements help you come to your conclusion?

4. "Milwaukee Police Once Queried Suspect" (on page 117) is an example of a feature story. What is the purpose of a feature story? Does this article achieve that purpose?

5. Identify each of the sources in "As Serial Killer Reaches Out, Fear Grips Wichita" (on page 146) as a primary or secondary source. Evaluate the reliability and credibility of each source. How does your evaluation of each source change your perspective on this article?

6. "The Serial Killer's Co-Author" (on page 180) is an example of an interview. What are the benefits of providing readers with direct quotes of an interviewed subject's speech? Is the subject of an interview always a reliable source?

7. What is the intention of "Do Serial Killers Just Stop? Yes, Sometimes" (on page 203)? How effectively does the piece achieve its purpose?

Citations

All citations in this list are formatted according to the Modern Language Association's (MLA) style guide.

BOOK CITATION

THE NEW YORK TIMES EDITORIAL STAFF. *Serial Killers: Jack the Ripper, Son of Sam and Others*. New York: New York Times Educational Publishing, 2019.

ONLINE ARTICLE CITATIONS

ALTER, ALEXANDRA. "Michelle McNamara Hunted, and Was Haunted by, the Golden State Killer." *The New York Times*, 15 Feb. 2018, https://www.nytimes.com/2018/02/15/books/michelle-mcnamara-patton-oswalt-book-serial-killer.html.

BARRON, JAMES. "Milwaukee Police Once Queried Suspect." *The New York Times*, 27 July 1991, https://www.nytimes.com/1991/07/27/us/milwaukee-police-once-queried-suspect.html.

BARRON, JAMES, AND MARY B. W. TABOR. "17 Killed, and a Life Is Searched for Clues." *The New York Times*, 4 Aug. 1991, https://www.nytimes.com/1991/08/04/us/17-killed-and-a-life-is-searched-for-clues.html.

BARRY, DAN, ET AL. "The Golden State Killer Left a Trail of Horror With Taunts and Guile." *The New York Times*, 28 Apr. 2018, https://www.nytimes.com/2018/04/28/us/golden-state-killer-joseph-deangelo.html.

BLUM, HOWARD. "The Suspect Is Quoted on Killings: 'It Was a Command ... I Had a Sign.'" *The New York Times*, 12 Aug. 1977, https://www.nytimes.com/1977/08/12/archives/new-jersey-pages-the-suspect-is-quoted-on-killings-it-was-a-command.html.

BLUM, HOWARD. "Who Is Really Behind That .44? Police Pursuing Many Theories." *The New York Times*, 3 Aug. 1977, https://www.nytimes.com/1977/08/03/archives/who-is-really-behind-that-44-police-pursuing-many-theories.html.

DAVEY, MONICA. "Arrest Is Made in Series of Killings in Kansas." *The New*

York Times, 27 Feb. 2005, https://www.nytimes.com/2005/02/27/us/arrest
-is-made-in-series-of-killings-in-kansas.html.

DAVEY, MONICA. "As Serial Killer Reaches Out, Fear Grips Wichita." *The New
York Times*, 2 Apr. 2004, https://www.nytimes.com/2004/04/02/us/as
-serial-killer-reaches-out-fear-grips-wichita.html.

DAVEY, MONICA. "Computer Disk Led to Arrest in Killings, Pastor Says." *The
New York Times*, 2 Mar. 2005, https://www.nytimes.com/2005/03/02/us
/computer-disk-led-to-arrest-in-killings-pastor-says.html.

DAVEY, MONICA. "Suspect in 10 Kansas Murders Lived an Intensely Ordinary Life."
The New York Times, 6 Mar. 2005, https://www.nytimes.com/2005/03/06
/us/suspect-in-10-kansas-murders-lived-an-intensely-ordinary-life.html.

GOLEMAN, DANIEL. "Clues to a Dark Nurturing Ground for One Serial Killer."
The New York Times, 7 Aug. 1991, https://www.nytimes.com/1991/08/07/us
/clues-to-a-dark-nurturing-ground-for-one-serial-killer.html.

HAAG, MATTHEW. "What We Know About Joseph DeAngelo, the Golden State
Killer Suspect." *The New York Times*, 26 Apr. 2018, https://www.nytimes.com
/2018/04/26/us/joseph-james-deangelo.html.

HAUSER, CHRISTINE. "Search for 'Golden State Killer' Leads to Arrest of Ex-Cop."
The New York Times, 25 Apr. 2018, https://www.nytimes.com/2018
/04/25/us/golden-state-killer-serial.html.

HOFFMAN, JAN. "Do Serial Killers Just Stop? Yes, Sometimes." *The New York
Times*, 26 Apr. 2018, https://www.nytimes.com/2018/04/26/health/serial
-killers-golden-state.html.

JOHNSON, DIRK. "Milwaukee Jury Says Dahmer Was Sane." *The New York
Times*, 16 Feb. 1992, https://www.nytimes.com/1992/02/16/us/milwaukee
-jury-says-dahmer-was-sane.html.

KIFNER, JOHN. "Man Who Killed 33 Is Executed in Illnois." *The New York
Times*, 10 May 1994, https://www.nytimes.com/1994/05/10/us/man-who
-killed-33-is-executed-in-illnois.html.

KNEELAND, DOUGLAS E. "4 More Bodies Found Under House of Contractor,
Bringing Total to 9." *The New York Times*, 27 Dec. 1978, https://www.nytimes
.com/1978/12/27/archives/4-more-bodies-found-under-house-of-contractor
-bringing-total-to-9.html.

KNEELAND, DOUGLAS E. "Parents of Missing Youths Hope, Fear — and Wait." *The
New York Times*, 31 Dec. 1978, https://www.nytimes.com/1978/12/31/archives
/parents-of-missing-youths-hope-fearand-wait-told-of-32-killings-not.html.

KNEELAND, DOUGLAS E. "Suspect in Mass Deaths Is Puzzle to All." *The New*

York Times, 10 Jan. 1979, https://www.nytimes.com/1979/01/10/archives /suspect-in-mass-deaths-is-puzzle-to-all-affable-driven-businessman.html.

KNEELAND, DOUGLAS E. "Suspect Pleads Not Guilty to 7 Murder Counts at Hearing on Sex Attacks." *The New York Times*, 11 Jan. 1979, https://www .nytimes.com/1979/01/11/archives/suspect-pleads-not-guilty-to-7-murder -counts-at-hearing-on-sex.html.

MCFADDEN, ROBERT D. "Suspect in 'Son of Sam' Murders Arrested in Yonkers." *The New York Times*, 11 Aug. 1977, https://www.nytimes.com/1977/08/11 /archives/suspect-in-son-of-sam-murders-arrested-in-yonkers-police-say .html.

MCFADDEN, ROBERT D. "Suspect Is Emerging as a Study in Extreme and Varied Contrast." *The New York Times*, 13 Aug. 1977, https://www.nytimes.com/1977/08/13 /archives/suspect-is-emerging-as-a-study-in-extreme-and-varied-contrast.html.

NAPOLITANO, JO. "Letter From Killer." *The New York Times*, 26 Mar. 2004, https://www.nytimes.com/2004/03/26/us/national-briefing-midwest -kansas-letter-from-killer.html.

THE NEW YORK TIMES. "Accused of Ten Murders" *The New York Times*, 26 July 1895, https://www.nytimes.com/1895/07/26/archives/accused-of -ten-murders-the-list-of-holmess-supposed-victims-grows.html.

THE NEW YORK TIMES. "Bodies Found at Illinois Suspect's House Total 21." *The New York Times*, 28 Dec. 1978, https://www.nytimes.com/1978/12/29 /archives/bodies-found-at-illinois-suspects-house-total-21-digging-to.html.

THE NEW YORK TIMES. "Bones of Holmes's Victims." *The New York Times*, 18 Sept. 1896, https://www.nytimes.com/1896/09/18/archives/bones-of -holmess-victims-dug-up-in-obedience-to-a-dream-near-the.html.

THE NEW YORK TIMES. "The Case Opened." *The New York Times*, 29 Oct. 1895, https://www.nytimes.com/1895/10/29/archives/the-case-opened-a-strong -plea-by-the-prisoner-for-a-postponement.html.

THE NEW YORK TIMES. "Dismay in Whitechapel; Two More Murdered Women Found." *The New York Times*, 1 Oct. 1888, https://www.nytimes.com/1888 /10/01/archives/dismay-in-whitechapel-two-more-murdered-women-found -one-nights-work.html.

THE NEW YORK TIMES. "Holmes Cool to the End."*The New York Times*, 8 May 1896, https://www.nytimes.com/1896/05/08/archives/holmes-cool-to-the -end-under-the-noose-he-says-he-only-killed-two.html.

THE NEW YORK TIMES. "Holmes Had Sharp Knives and Saws; They Were Sharpened Just Before Howard Pietzel Died." *The New York Times*, 3 Sept.

1895, https://www.nytimes.com/1895/09/03/archives/holmes-had-sharp
-knives-and-saws-they-were-sharpened-just-before.html.

THE NEW YORK TIMES. "Holmes Is Found Guilty." *The New York Times*,
2 Nov. 1895, https://www.nytimes.com/1895/11/03/archives/holmes-is
-found-guilty-the-jury-reaches-its-verdict-on-the-first.html.

THE NEW YORK TIMES. "Holmes Killed Pietzel." *The New York Times*, 18 July
1895, https://www.nytimes.com/1895/07/18/archives/holmes-killed-pietzel
-will-be-tried-at-philadelphia-for-the-murder.html.

THE NEW YORK TIMES. "Jack the Ripper Again." *The New York Times*, 13 Feb.
1890, https://www.nytimes.com/1891/02/13/archives/jack-the-ripper-again
-another-woman-murdered-and-her-body-mangled.html.

THE NEW YORK TIMES. "Judgment on Son of Sam." *The New York Times*,
11 May 1978, https://www.nytimes.com/1978/05/11/archives/judgment
-on-son-of-sam.html.

THE NEW YORK TIMES. "Letter from Berkowitz Says He Killed 6 Persons." *The
New York Times*, 20 Sept. 1977, https://www.nytimes.com/1977/09/20/archives
/letter-from-berkowitz-says-he-killed-6-persons.html.

THE NEW YORK TIMES. "The London Paranoiac." *The New York Times*, 8 Oct. 1888,
https://www.nytimes.com/1888/10/08/archives/the-london-paranoiac.html.

THE NEW YORK TIMES. "May Be Charged with Murder." *The New York Times*,
19 Nov. 1894, https://www.nytimes.com/1894/11/19/archives/may-be
-charged-with-murder-conspiracy-to-swindle-an-insurance.html.

THE NEW YORK TIMES. "Police Get a 2d Note Signed by 'Son of Sam' in .44-
Caliber Killings." *The New York Times*, 3 June 1977, https://www.nytimes
.com/1977/06/03/archives/police-get-a-2d-note-signed-by-son-of-sam-in
-44caliber-killings.html.

THE NEW YORK TIMES. " 'Son of Sam' Adds Four Names in New Letter,
Police Disclose." *The New York Times*, 6 June 1977, https://www.nytimes
.com/1977/06/06/archives/son-of-sam-adds-four-names-in-new-letter
-police-disclose.html.

THE NEW YORK TIMES. "Still Another Victim" *The New York Times*, 29 July
1895, https://www.nytimes.com/1895/07/29/archives/where-is-mh-cole
-he-is-thought-to-have-been-one-of-holmess-victims.html.

THE NEW YORK TIMES. "A Warning to Whitechapel." *The New York Times*, 2 Oct. 1890,
https://www.nytimes.com/1890/10/02/archives/a-warning-to-whitechapel.html.

THE NEW YORK TIMES. "The Whitechapel Crime; No Clue to the Perpetrator
of the Latest Murder." *The New York Times*, 18 July 1889, https://www

.nytimes.com/1889/07/18/archives/the-whitechapel-crime-no-clue-to-the -perpetrator-of-the-latest.html.

THE NEW YORK TIMES. "Whitechapel Startled By a Fourth Murder." *The New York Times*, 9 Sept. 1888, https://timesmachine.nytimes.com/timesmachine /1888/09/09/106332341.html.

THE NEW YORK TIMES. "Whitechapel's Mysterious Murderer." *The New York Times*, 4 Sept. 1888, https://timesmachine.nytimes.com/timesmachine /1888/09/04/106191687.html.

THE NEW YORK TIMES. "The Williams Girls' Fate; Probably Murdered and Burned by Holmes in Chicago." *The New York Times*, 21 July 1895, https:// www.nytimes.com/1895/07/21/archives/the-williams-girls-fate-probably -murdered-and-burned-by-holmes-at.html.

PACE, ERIC. "Cry for Help Wakes Up a Brooklyn Neighborhood." *The New York Times*, 1 Aug. 1977, https://www.nytimes.com/1977/08/01/archives/cry-for -help-wakes-up-a-brooklyn-neighborhood.html.

RICH, FRANK. "Loving Jeffrey Dahmer." *The New York Times*, 17 Mar. 1994, https:// www.nytimes.com/1994/03/17/opinion/journal-loving-jeffrey-dahmer.html.

SHEPPARD, NATHANIEL, JR. "Gacy Is Found Guilty of Killing 33, Record for U.S. Mass Murder." *The New York Times*, 13 Mar. 1980, https://www.nytimes .com/1980/03/13/archives/gacy-is-found-guilty-of-killing-33-record-for-us -mass-murder-gacy.html.

SHTEIR, RACHEL. "The Serial Killer's Co-Author." *The New York Times*, 15 Sept. 2016, https://www.nytimes.com/2016/09/15/magazine/the-serial-killers -co-author.html.

TERRY, DON. "Jeffrey Dahmer, Multiple Killer, Is Bludgeoned to Death in Prison." *The New York Times*, 29 Nov. 1994, https://www.nytimes.com/1994/11/29/us /jeffrey-dahmer-multiple-killer-is-bludgeoned-to-death-in-prison.html.

WILGOREN, JODI. "Kansas Suspect Pleads Guilty in 10 Murders." *The New York Times*, 28 June 2005, https://www.nytimes.com/2005/06/28/us/kansas -suspect-pleads-guilty-in-10-murders.html.

WILGOREN, JODI. "10 Life Terms for B.T.K. Strangler as Anguished Families Condemn Him in Court." *The New York Times*, 19 Aug. 2005, https://www .nytimes.com/2005/08/19/us/10-life-terms-for-btk-strangler-as-anguished -families-condemn-him-in.html.

WILSON, MICHAEL. "Shadows at Home: Living Where B.T.K. Killed." *The New York Times*, 29 June 2005, https://www.nytimes.com/2005/06/29/us/shadows -at-home-living-where-btk-killed.html.

Index

This book is current up until the time of printing. For the most up-to-date reporting, visit www.nytimes.com.